ARTIFICIAL INTELLIGENCE

FOR

FINANCE EXECUTIVES

ALEXIS BESSE

Edited by Joanna Pyke
Typeset by pblpublishing.co.uk
Cover designed by Vanessa Mendozzi

Published by Qbridge Ltd
Kemp House, 160 City Road
London, United Kingdom, EC1V 2NX
publisher@qbridgeplatform.com

First edition published 2021

CONTENTS

PART TWO: AI IN ACTION

PREFACE

"I learned very early the difference between knowing
the name of something and knowing something."
Richard P. Feynman

MOTIVATION FOR THE BOOK AND BOOK STRUCTURE

I remember it was about a decade ago that colleagues started asking me about ways to build tools to make their decisions more data-driven and less subjective. At the time, I was in charge of financial engineering for a large American investment bank. Times should have been good, but instead they were very challenging, thanks to the Great Financial Crisis. I wanted to be better prepared for the next crisis and started tinkering with what would nowadays be called a robo-advisor. The question I wanted to answer was: how could we make the whole investment process more robust, and less driven by emotions which ultimately lead to bad choices? In the process, I was happy to reconnect with my graduate studies in mathematical optimisation and statistical inference. I wanted my algorithm to incorporate the work that Daniel Kahneman was doing to extend his *prospect theory* to cover a wide range of human biases, in particular those that related to the investment process. It was my first attempt at building an automated system that could learn investment rules and asset allocation from the data itself and embed domain knowledge within it as well.

A decade ago, there was not much talk of artificial intelligence or machine learning within the financial community. Since then, I have had countless debates with friends, colleagues, and business acquaintances from all financial disciplines about the best use of data as a complement to human expertise. These discussions pushed me to start thinking about the transformative trend that we are experiencing and how to frame it.

Now, times have changed and Artificial Intelligence (AI) and Big Data are part of every conversation. But something does not feel right. Data and analytics initiatives are often pushed to technology and data science teams with little involvement from front-line executives. No financial services executive would ignore the principles of sound risk management or capital adequacy. So why should such a profound transformation in data processing – the AI revolution – be handled solely by the technical staff? It should be embraced by everyone, whether on the technology side or on the business side. This book is my contribution to this process. It is my response to a question I get asked often by executives within the industry – How much do I need to know to manage and guide an AI initiative in my company?

This book contains three sections. Firstly, I set the scene with the key concepts and the common misconceptions regarding the artificial intelligence revolution and why now is the time to care. Then I get to the heart of the matter where I review the business side, the industry trends which align with this transformation, use cases, associated risks and more. Finally, I end with a few technical chapters. I believe that understanding the technology is critical to being impactful, but I appreciate that some readers may be put off by this. My only hope is that, once you have learned enough of the business potential, you will be tempted to know more about the *how*.

My ambition for this book is to help you to develop an intuition for the field. Knowledge is key but building intuition is even more powerful, especially in order to be creative. The mathematician Henri Poincaré put it eloquently: "It is by logic that we prove, but by intuition that we discover. To know how to criticise is good, to know how to create is better." In fact, this is an opinion that is at odds with the French way of thinking. French education tends to favour theoretical rigour over experimentation and intuitive sense. I understood what Poincaré meant when I discovered the "Feynman Lectures on Physics" as a physics undergraduate. Suddenly, a whole new world appeared beyond the dry equations – involving experiments, observations and feeling things. By design, I have not included a single equation and barely any mathematical references in my book. It has made my life harder when writing it, but it has also pushed me to clarify my thoughts in plain English, which I think is ultimately beneficial for the reader. Despite the absence of mathematical equations, I have still attempted to give you a glimpse of some of the incredible complexity in the field, and to share a bit of the passion that I have developed for the discipline.

WHO IS THIS BOOK FOR?

Ideally, I would like my core readers to be the ones who cannot stand AI. Maybe because they hear it everywhere these days and it sounds like just another buzzword. Or maybe they just do not believe in it. After all, finance has seen its fair share of innovations that failed to live up to the hype. If this describes your attitude towards AI, I hope that you grant me the opportunity to convince you of the truly transformative nature of the field.

Of course, I also welcome business readers who are already inclined towards AI. Maybe you just want to learn more about all the practical ways in which you can be part of this revolution. Or maybe you wish to better understand how it could fit within your specific area of expertise. Here, I hope to cover enough vantage points – the practical applications from both a business and an organisational standpoint, the possible risks associated with the technology, the tools that can be used, and most importantly the concepts underpinning the whole discipline. In this manner, if I can help you to develop enough of an intuition for the way that AI may be applied, you can become a true agent of change within your organisation. Fostering creativity in solving business problems is all I wish for.

Beyond the sceptics and the ambassadors, I would be delighted to attract readers from other business areas as well. Finance can act as a domain to showcase concrete applications, away from the media hype of conversational assistants and image tagging software. My ambition would be to evidence the breadth of the technology and the many ways in which it can augment our capabilities as human beings, working alongside us, and certainly not replacing us. I believe we have just scratched the surface of the technology's potential, and its current limitations are mostly due to our lack of imagination. All it takes is a bit of confidence and ingenuity to extend its boundaries.

WHAT IS THIS BOOK AND WHAT IT IS NOT?

This book simply contains my own views as a practitioner in both AI and finance. I am not an AI researcher. Undoubtedly, I have a deep interest in academic research, especially when it helps solve problems that we have previously struggled with, or sometimes just for the beauty of a new algorithmic architecture. But I am most impressed with new practical applications when there is a perfect alignment between the framing of the business problem and the technological solution.

In that sense, this book is not an exhaustive review of the field of AI or machine learning. The reality is that this is now impossible to achieve in a concise manner. Any review would require at least a thousand pages to do justice to the field and it would need to be updated almost constantly. Once again, I am more interested in helping you, the reader, to understand the key concepts. The rest of the concepts can be explored over time as you dig deeper into the field. I hope that this book will trigger an interest in you to know more and to keep learning – as the machines do.

PART ONE
THE AI CONTEXT

1

PROLOGUE

A TALE OF TWO ASSET MANAGERS

If you are interested in private credit, you might have come across two investment managers, Red Mountain Credit Opportunities and Blue Horizon Credit Partners.[1] They are both active in selecting credit assets, or more specifically small-size loans to individuals and businesses, for their large and highly diversified investment portfolios. They have embraced the opportunities of recent years, a combination of new lenders and an abundance of data, to help with the investment process. They can easily be classified as quantitative credit funds, and they look so similar from the outside that they are often compared to each other.

Potential investors often make parallels between the two companies. For instance, when Blue Horizon invests with a new lender, observers look for signs of interest at Red Mountain. To most investors, they seem indistinguishable. However, the reality could not be further from the truth. They both use data in the form of loan tapes and they both invest in credit assets, but that is where the resemblance ends.

---

1 These two companies are totally fictitious, but any resemblance to actual organisations may *not* be coincidental

Over the years, Red Mountain has built a team of credit analysts and portfolio managers with incredible industry experience. They have an in-depth knowledge of both the trends and the process to invest in the asset class. They have invested heavily in a credit scoring system that can grade loans to fit the portfolio. It is truly the backbone of the whole investment process. The team has crafted complex heuristics to select the best assets. These rules are really the transcription in formulas of the investment team's knowledge. With years of experience embedded in the system, it is the key selling point to new investors. There is undoubtedly a robust investment framework. Rules and heuristics encoded from the best credit professionals are all in there. For instance, they like to maintain a broad diversification across geographies and business sectors or types of consumers. Their rules state that they prefer moderate leverage, good balance-sheet at the individual or business level, etc.

On the other hand, Blue Horizon started from first principles. Investment rules had to be learned over time from the data itself – from a repository of millions of loans with their credit and non-credit attributes, as well as their lifetime performance. The team also spent significant time enriching the loan tapes with relevant public datasets and macro-economic variables to form a comprehensive line-by-line view of the assets. The philosophy behind it was to avoid any *a priori*. Of course, the portfolio managers were vital in framing the problem and designing the data inputs to feed the system. But, it was essential to Blue Horizon not to limit the space of possibilities. It was a question of what the data tells us, rather than relying on *a priori* human expertise. In building sophisticated algorithms, the engineers were able to capture complex interactions between variables. They noticed that the response from the change of a given feature in the dataset was not constant in terms of credit score. They also learned that some variables were crucial in explaining the credit quality of certain assets, but other variables were at play for different groups of loans. These were already two sources of non-linearity. Lastly, because the investment team did not rely on already written rules, the engineers developed a whole corpus of tools to understand the algorithmic decisions better.

I am sure you have guessed by now that Blue Horizon is using *Artificial Intelligence* (AI), while Red Mountain is not. The difference is fundamental. In the case of Red Mountain, constructing rules is hard, messy, unreliable, and, crucially, highly subjective and biased. Automating the work of human assessors is not straightforward. In particular, investment professionals might disagree, and conflicts may arise. Sometimes it is the narrative developed by the portfolio manager that prevails. In the absence of well-identified facts, it is the story around a particular phenomenon that usually wins. In this process, there is no ground truth, so it is by definition subjective. It also relies on the fact that the same paradigm still holds. Lessons learned from the past form the basis of the rule system and change is difficult to incorporate. Finally, it is culturally challenging. The human is alone in the decision process. It creates a binary outcome – either they are right and praised or they are wrong and quickly discredited.

Blue Horizon, instead, built a process, a data-driven machine. Any portfolio manager can run multiple models at once and assess their predictions. It is as simple as tweaking a few parameters. The engineers can continually enrich the algorithms with new data sources too. Onboarding new lenders is easy as the process is already coded. It is less susceptible to biases because the insight is driven by the data collected. The team can review multiple business opportunities much more quickly, rather than waiting for weeks or months to conduct a costly due diligence. From a culture standpoint, it is more fulfilling as engineers and portfolio managers work towards a common goal of understanding changing markets. Also, humans are now augmented by the machines, instead of solely relying on their intuition. For the organisation, there is a broader vision too. In this data-driven world, it is becoming a fiduciary duty for an asset manager to use the available data in the best possible way, through the most advanced technology. That fact cannot be ignored any longer.

But, at no time is the difference more prevalent than through a market crisis. In such a case, Red Mountain needs to conduct emergency meetings to evaluate possible changes in the rules. However, the only available tool is to scale back, to use more conservative thresholds on the scorecards. Their hands are tied by the rigid rules in place. And then later, the team needs to go back to the drawing board to figure out what can be learned from the crisis. And the cacophony starts again. For Blue Horizon, there are several tools at their disposal. They can change the training period of the models to overweight the more recent past. They can rerun models to see the changes arising from the crisis. They may add alternative data to better capture in real-time the specific drivers of the crisis too. And lastly and most fundamentally, they can use their tools to forensically understand the model predictions, rather than being left in the dark.

Over time, costs at Red Mountain are grinding higher. Maintaining the rules is a challenge. There is no built-in mechanism to update the rulebook. More resources are needed to make the system respond to market changes, and the whole process becomes chaotic. Grand plans to review and simplify the investment guidelines are always postponed, as it is a massive undertaking. In the meantime, it requires a lot of management time. It is always a lengthy process of approval to make any change as any amendment feels somewhat subjective. Also, market opportunities are missed. It is too costly to onboard new loan originators. True diversification in the portfolio suffers – both from the inability to explore new combinations of loan attributes and from the small number of lenders.

Blue Horizon enjoys better diversification on these two metrics. It can explore a broader universe of possibilities. Thanks to the system's learning abilities, the company spends less time updating it. The firm benefits from high operating leverage and can focus on growing its business on both lending and marketing fronts.

The premise in the AI approach, embraced by Blue Horizon, is that good credit performance cannot be synthesised through simple heuristics. The AI system has a built-in adaptive system, can learn complex combinations of variables, and is likely to explore a more extensive set of combinations associated with good credit performance. In simple words, Red Mountain equips its portfolio managers with inflexible automatons, while Blue Horizon builds an evolvable learning system.

This book explores the Blue Horizon approach in finance and, in particular, some of the subtler traits associated with AI – autonomous learning, data structures acquisition, learning framework, built-in adaptability, etc.

2

WHAT IS AI IN FINANCE?

"I invented the term artificial intelligence. I invented it because we had to do something when we were trying to get money for a summer study in 1956."

John McCarthy

Artificial Intelligence sells. AI has become so hyped these days that it needs to be part of any commercial offering. In a startling large-scale study[2] in 2019, 44% of startups classified as AI startups[3] did not show any evidence of "AI material to a company's value proposition". And the reason might be simple. For startup and growth companies, there is evidence that invoking AI helps command larger funding rounds or is associated with increased valuations later in their development.

Even for large organisations in finance, such as a bank or an asset manager, AI – or its derivative forms of digital, digital transformation, big data, machine learning, data analytics – needs to find its place in the investor presentation. For the leadership team, AI conveys the message of an innovative company on a mission to future-proof their operations. It is a required placeholder for many companies before they can

2 (MMC Ventures 2019)

3 The study reviewed 2,830 purported AI startups, in the 13 EU countries most active in AI

assess what technologies to use in their core activities, how to use them, or how much to invest in them. Whether management believes in it or not, these companies have to adopt AI due to competitive pressures.

More worryingly, AI has become a fancy synonym of *data analysis*. If you use data or some form of quantitative analysis in your business processes, if you collect data or if you plan to collect data, you are doing AI. With such a broad definition, pretty much any project in modern finance qualifies as AI.

AI, A MISNOMER

The very reason that the confusion exists between various quantitative methods may be found at the beginning of the AI journey. *Artificial Intelligence* was coined by John McCarthy in 1955[4] in a different historical context. A few years later, Marvin Minsky, another founding father of AI,[5] gave this definition: "AI is the science of making machines capable of performing tasks that would require intelligence if done by humans."

It seems clear from this definition that AI is involved with systems that *appear intelligent*. On that basis and even before knowing what *intelligence* is, it excludes most quantitative techniques, which merely apply a set of predetermined computing rules.

However, this is not useful terminology from a practical standpoint. It shifts the definition of AI to the definition of *intelligence*.[6] Here,

---

4 (The Lighthill debate on Artificial Intelligence: "The general purpose robot is a mirage" 1973)

5 The founding fathers of AI are considered to be: John McCarthy, Marvin Minsky, Allen Newell, and Herbert Simon

6 For a more advanced study of intelligence and how to build fair intelligence comparisons between human beings and machines, I refer the reader to François Chollet's excellent essay: (F. Chollet 2019)

note that intelligence refers to *human intelligence*. In that context, two important aspects are worth mentioning. The first observation is that, despite what we think about our intelligence's general nature, it is somewhat limited. There certainly are other forms of intelligence to which the human race is not exposed. *Intelligence* in AI has, therefore, a meaning purely in reference to the world we live in, experience, and feel. The second observation is that what AI really attempts is to reach or exceed human performance at specific tasks that we, humans, are deemed to perform using our *intelligence*. This is why we often hear about *narrow* intelligence if it covers a single or narrow set of tasks – the current state of AI – as opposed to a more *general* intelligence that would encompass a much wider scope of applications, which is the goal of *Artificial General Intelligence* (AGI).

In this debate, it might be easier to define what properties this human intelligence – that AI is trying to mimic or surpass – exhibits. As thinking humans, we possess the ability to reason, solve problems, perceive, speak, and understand a language. In 1950, Alan Turing proposed the Turing test[7] as the ultimate experiment to assess whether a particular system had reached human intelligence. Not surprisingly, the test involves a conversation. The command of a language and its intricacies in terms of meaning are intuitively associated with intelligent behaviours. There are multiple versions of the test, but in its original form, it involves an evaluator, a machine and a human being. Through text only, the evaluator interrogates both the machine and the human. If the evaluator cannot reliably distinguish the machine from the human, the machine is deemed to have passed the test of reaching human intelligence. It is worth noting that the accuracy of the answers to the questions does not matter. So again, the test is concerned with

---

7 (Turing 2009)

identifying intelligent behaviour rather than defining what true intelligence is.

In the same line of thinking, you might have heard of the *AI effect*. It is a widespread human bias, whereby we, humans, tend to exclude from intelligent behaviours whatever task machines have already been able to achieve. Douglas Hofstadter rather eloquently illustrated the effect as: "AI is whatever has not been done yet."[8] So, we can reject checkers, chess, and now the game of Go, where AI systems are already unbeatable by human players. However, it is not because we figured out the source code enabling a machine to perform brilliantly at a particular task that this does not qualify as intelligent. To close this digression, Fred Reed, reflecting on the defeat of Gary Kasparov by IBM's Deep Blue, wittily wrote: "A problem that proponents of AI regularly face is this: When we know how a machine does something 'intelligent,' it ceases to be regarded as intelligent. If I beat the world's chess champion, I'd be regarded as highly bright."[9]

THE PILLARS OF AI

AI is not automation, which is an entire field by itself in business processing. AI needs to display what we consider as intelligent behaviours. As such, there are no clear boundaries to the field, but for all intents and purposes, modern AI has become synonymous with *machine learning* (ML). Computer vision or natural language processing (NLP) are sometimes considered sub-fields of AI, distinct from machine learning, but this is questionable. Only *robotics* – as the field concerned with replicating human actions – can be considered a separate area

8 (Hofstadter 1979)
9 (Promise of AI not so bright 2006)

of AI, with only the parts tasked with information processing using machine learning techniques. Also, robotics involves other disciplines like mechanical and electronic engineering, which are well understood as being separate from machine learning.

So, in the rest of the book, it is easier – and historically accurate – to see AI and machine learning as interchangeable terms. There have been periods where AI used alternative techniques to machine learning. Symbolic AI, from the beginning of AI in the mid-1950s through to expert systems in the 1980s, attempted to replicate human intelligence by using logic and search algorithms. With the dramatic increase in computing capacity and until the mid-2000s, brute-force search was employed as a way to solve the more complex problems in AI.

However, for more than 20 years, machine learning has been the dominant, and now the only technique for solving AI. Acknowledging this fact helps us make a significant step towards understanding the technology. While, on paper, AI encompasses a wide range of cognitive traits associated with human intelligence, like reasoning, perception, etc., the ability for a machine to *learn* is what best defines modern AI. Algorithms used in AI have at their core a mechanism to learn, to learn autonomously from data.

MACHINE LEARNING

Learning can be achieved through various means, so a detour through how we, human beings, learn as toddlers might be helpful. In these early years of our lives, most of the learning is done at home or school by showing and naming objects, actions, etc. Through repetition, children learn to understand the critical characteristics of an object. Over time, they are able to recognise a similar object, even if it is not precisely the one that they have seen before. Rather fortunately, this learning process is called *supervised learning* in AI. Note that this is not to be confused with rote learning. Children learn conceptually what the object is, hence their ability to tag the object correctly when shown a new instance of that object. It is not just about bringing the record of that object back from memory.

Another form of learning is when children interact with their environment in an unsupervised manner. So-called *unsupervised learning* typically involves recognising a structure in the objects they are in contact with. Without being directed, being able to group toys by shape or colour is a typical unsupervised learning task. The key point is that there is no known classification of the objects to the children. Through a – yet undefined – learning mechanism, a structure is found according to which objects could be clustered. In business, real-life examples of unsupervised tasks are certainly more complex, as the hidden structure is unlikely to be that obvious to a human. However, the complexity of the task is probably similarly high in the mind of a toddler.

A third well-known learning mechanism, named *reinforcement learning*, which is, in the current state of affairs, the least common, is through *rewards*. Again, children interact freely with their environment, take actions, and at some point, they might receive a reward – or possibly a punishment – from their parents or teachers. Through the repetition of a series of actions, and their ultimate associated reward, children learn certain behaviours.

Of course, these learning mechanisms that children resort to are different from how machine learning implements them, but they are close enough as illustrations. One aspect where children are vastly superior to a machine in their learning abilities is the amount of training they need. Humans learn extremely fast compared to computers. Only a few examples (or samples) are required before children can recognise a similar object in a new situation. We will see

WHAT IS AI IN FINANCE?

later that machines ideally need a lot of data to learn patterns, which has profound implications in the world of finance.

Understanding these learning mechanisms brings us a step closer to grasping what machine learning can achieve in terms of practical applications. In supervised learning, we saw, in the case of a toddler learning, that samples (or examples) needed to be named, for instance by a parent. For a machine, the mechanism is very similar. Such a task is called a *classification* task and is among the most common use cases of machine learning. The purpose of the algorithm is to be able to classify a new piece of data correctly. The process is the following. The machine is fed with training samples, i.e. examples of data that have been first labelled as belonging to a given class. For instance, in our previous case of the AI credit manager, these are individual loans – for which the machine knows if they ultimately repaid or defaulted. The two classes are *repaid* and *defaulted*, and the purpose of the classifier is to predict if a new, unseen, loan should be classified in one or the other class. To achieve this, the learning mechanism involves an optimisation process that tries to amend the weights (or the importance) associated with the various characteristics of the sample loans. That process continues until the misclassification rate is low enough.

In summary, in a classification task, in supervised learning, the data is labelled (we know the true classes). The algorithm updates its parameters through iterative steps to classify the training data correctly. For instance, if we want to predict whether the equity market will go *up* or *down* the following day, based on several features describing the market, we will build a similar classification model, where the two classes are *market up* and *market down*. The model will be trained over a number of trading days to correctly predict the next day's performance.

15

UNDERSTANDING AI THROUGH AN ENGINEERING LENS

I chose to describe and explain AI in terms of engineering techniques, rather than listing its possible applications. This presentation choice is indeed much more efficient, as understanding what underpins these algorithms and their associated learning techniques is much quicker than reviewing all the potential applications. Applications in AI usually involve a relatively small set of technologies, or at least, small when compared to its applications across disciplines and business areas.

Extensively reviewing concrete applications would be a daunting task. Whether it is autonomous exploration or intelligent control in robotics, object recognition or image classification and captioning in computer vision, speech recognition or generation in speech processing, machine translation or text classification in natural language processing, time series prediction in economics and finance, the application space is vast, but with significant overlap between use cases.

THE ESSENCE OF AI

Despite covering a vast area of applications and techniques, AI, in its modern incarnation, has a few key characteristics. It needs data, and the more the better. At an abstract level, it is a form of advanced pattern recognition, from which it attempts to make accurate predictions.

So, the whole field of AI is concerned with building algorithms that can perform well on unseen data, an ability known as *generalisation*. The ultimate goal is for the models to *generalise well*, and they attempt to do so through learning. In learning possibly intricate patterns, AI models extract the hidden structure of data, enabling them to make inferences on new experiences.

A BRIEF HISTORY OF AI IN FINANCE AND ELSEWHERE

The history of AI has been marked by periods of high hopes, a faith in the future, and other periods of disappointment and failed attempts. Since the classical age, human beings have aspired to create mechanical devices – the early version of robots – that could perform tasks that only humans could do.[10] Over the centuries that followed, philosophers theorised that machines could do some form of reasoning, inspired by progress in logic. Also, as a discipline drawing inputs from multiple scientific fields, AI benefited from the advances in areas like statistics, mathematics, logic, and philosophy. For example, the *Bayes' theorem* in the 1760s was an important discovery with modern implications in Bayesian inference – whereby the model's beliefs are updated when exposed to additional data.

But, it was only in the 1940s and 1950s that AI was expressed in its modern form, with the possibility of *thinking machines*, exhibiting human intelligence, as evidenced in the work of Alan Turing.[11] This coincided with the advent of the first computers. In 1956, the field of AI was officially born at the "Dartmouth Summer Research Project on Artificial Intelligence."[12] However, that conference fell short of expectations. There was not much agreement about techniques and directions to solve these problems, but it laid the groundwork for future research. Interestingly, the initial conference proposal lists very similar questions to the ones that are still being asked today, around natural language, neuron nets, self-improvement, or randomness. It was truly visionary, and it is still inspirational to researchers to the present day.

10 For instance, Aristotle imagined in Politics the end of slavery with instruments performing their own work, by command or intelligent behaviour. See (The Politics of Aristotle. 1885)

11 (Turing 2009)

12 (McCarthy, et al. 1955)

The first working version of a neural network was the Perceptron, invented by Frank Rosenblatt in 1958, and inspired by the information processing in the brain. By analogy to the brain, the architecture of the Perceptron involves neurons that receive an input (electrical signal in the case of the brain) from other neurons. Such signals to the neuron are then summed up with certain weights that need to be learned – in the brain, synapses play that role with variable connection strengths. If a certain threshold is reached, the neuron is activated, and that information is passed through the network.

In the word of finance, companies became interested after WWII in the prospect of automation when analysing the growing amounts of data in the banking, accounting, and auditing sectors. Later and until the 1980s, *expert systems* became ubiquitous, especially in financial planning. These systems could take into account the balance-sheet of a family, its finances, goals and aspirations, and use thousands of encoded rules from experts in domains like accounting, taxation, laws, investment products and insurance to build affordable, comprehensive financial plans.[13] On the face of it, these systems appear to be much more sophisticated than modern-day robo-advisors.

These expert systems became dominant in the field of AI across industries and reflected the fundamental differences in the approach between *symbolic AI* and *connectionism*. The connectionist method (now called *neural networks*) is bottom-up and attempts to mimic the brain's information processing. For its proponents, the key to human intelligence resides in these particular low-level architectures and their learning mechanism from data. On the contrary, symbolic AI and its implementations in expert systems are all about encoding human expert knowledge into the machine

13 (Phillips, Nielson and Brown 1992)

through a series of interrogations. For the symbolists, with sufficient care, it is possible to *download* top-down, human intelligence.

With the pre-eminence of expert systems, AI and machine learning diverged. It was only later, in the 1990s, that machine learning would become again the workhorse of AI with its improved learning algorithms (including *backpropagation* discovered in the 1970s). In the 1980s and 1990s, the most severe *AI winter* took place. Expert systems did not deliver as expected. With their numerous explicit rules, they were too complex to maintain and did not generalise well when exposed to new data. Funding dried up and symbolic AI slowly disappeared as a field of AI research.

The advent of the internet, the growing supply of digital data, and exponentially improving computational power[14] put neural networks back on the map from the late 1990s onwards. And the past ten years have been all about *deep learning* – neural networks with multiple layers of neurons – with astonishing breakthroughs in language processing, computer vision, board games, etc. In finance, the most crucial development was the birth of the quant funds, which use a variety of quantitative methods, including machine learning.

14 (Moore's law 2020)

3

AI MYTHS THAT HAMPER AI ADOPTION

"Unless there is an obvious reason to do otherwise, most of us passively accept decision problems as they are framed and therefore rarely have an opportunity to discover the extent to which our preferences are frame-bound rather than reality-bound."

Daniel Kahneman

When it comes to tackling significant problems, AI adoption in finance has been surprisingly slow compared to other industries. One explanation is that finance and science are worlds apart. It is true that finance deals with numbers on a constant basis, but only in very limited areas has the quantitative side been a driving force. Finance is supported by quantitative analysis – and to a lesser extent, technology – but it has never been highly regarded by the real dealmakers. It is just a means to an end. Early in my career, I learned that, even in the highly quantitative field of derivatives, the quants devising the models were definitely not at the top of the pecking order. The dealing, the markets, were where the action was.

In that context of a certain disdain for analytical details, AI in finance suffers from deeply rooted beliefs about what it is, and these hinder its progress. There is widespread ignorance about the technology and what it can achieve. Coupled with that is a fear of the unknown, not dissimilar to what we have seen across other periods of technological change. Surely machines cannot really be thinking? It is more reassuring to dismiss the technology altogether and re-establish the pre-eminence of the human race. After all, our beloved field of finance is not that simple that it can be handled by computers.

AI = BIG DATA

For instance, AI is constantly associated – if not as a synonym – with *big data*. As a matter of fact, these terms are interchangeably used in corporate communications. And maintaining that confusion is not helpful.

When it comes to big data, a statistic by IBM is probably the most often cited: 90% of today's data in the world has been created in the past two years alone.[15] We all have this feeling of a data deluge, and AI should be our saviour. That is partly true, but not particularly in finance. Yes, AI needs data; it cannot learn if it cannot consume data. But, the vast majority of AI problems in finance do not qualify as big data. The volume of data beyond which you are in big data territory keeps getting larger and larger, as computing power increases. Most datasets in finance do not come close to this.

Big data is, first and foremost, the field of computer science where parallel computing is needed. It is primarily a data processing consideration. With vast datasets, handling data sequentially is

15 (IBM Marketing Cloud 2017)

no longer an option. It could be because it is not technically feasible, or due to the limited capacity of servers, or just because it is too expensive or slow to do so. For example, in many real-time applications, response time is crucial.

In finance, very few disciplines have this abundance of data. In some areas of retail banking, where clients' touchpoints are many, advanced data processing might be required. Also, in high-frequency trading, when dealing with tick-level data across an entire market, the volume of data is a challenge in itself. An exchange, collecting pre-trade and trading data, is in that category too. Coping with such a large amount of data has other implications also. It requires rethinking traditional ways to acquire data, store it, analyse it, visualise it, retrieve it, etc. But for the most part, financial datasets are not big data.

Finance not being in big data territory is not an advantage, but a disadvantage. More data is almost always the best way to improve predictive capability. Collecting data trumps refining the algorithm. In a famous paper, Microsoft's researchers[16] proved that point:[17] as data size increases, different models tend to converge in terms of performance. Also, the issue of smaller datasets is that it tends to create higher rates of *false discovery*. With fewer samples, it is easier to *overfit* the data and see patterns that do not exist in reality. In particular, when there are many possible explanatory variables, it is easy to combine them to explain a given output, even if the explanation is dubious.

And this is the tragedy of financial datasets. We cannot collect more data. We cannot create more trading days;[18] we cannot generate more

16 (Banko and Brill 2001)

17 It is important to note that their experiment was conducted on a particular task, *natural language disambiguation*

18 More on this later: the area of creating synthetic datasets is promising in finance

transactions, companies, securities, or clients. And if you think about it, the typical size of datasets is small in finance. When working on an investment strategy on a major equity index, you have access to only 2,500 trading days over a ten-year period. You probably do not want to go back in time much further given the changing market infrastructure. Moving to intraday data means 35,000 periods of 30 minutes. Is it even relevant to look at such a frequency given your investment horizon? You will just end up with many overlapping periods, and in any case, you are still far from the realm of big data. In most other finance applications, the typical number of rows in a dataset is in the tens of thousands, or possibly in the millions, but never in the billions. Sometimes people talk about data observations, the product of the number of rows by the number of columns in a dataset. That is a more significant number, but it still does not hide the fact that it is not large by any means.

There is also another argument, here, when identifying AI with big data. Big data – possibly on purpose – gives the impression that it is all about data. It feels as if it is just possible to solve business problems with data. If an organisation produces data, that should be enough to create value. We talk a lot these days about *monetising data assets*. I certainly like the term, but it implies that there is value in data at a general level. But, it is not sufficient to just talk about data in a business presentation. One needs to make an effort to spell out how we can *monetise* that data. AI is tasked with making that happen: the organisation has access to relevant data, has a business problem to solve and AI techniques to convert that value. It is all about extracting information from data. So, we should collectively stop talking about big data in finance, and start to explain how AI can help in a concrete manner.

MACHINE LEARNING IS JUST LINEAR REGRESSION

There is another cliché that comes up regularly in discussions with professionals in finance. It is that learning from data ultimately boils down to *linear regression*. Making predictions can be called machine learning, but when implemented, in the mind of people, it is just linear regression. This is not unexpected, given that most econometric models use linear regression, and are indeed useful for understanding relationships between economic variables and to make high-level forecasts. Also, the whole field of supervised learning, in machine learning, when dealing with real-valued outputs, is called *regression* (though not linear).

This is where the ignorance of the discipline reveals itself. A quick review of the field reveals that model architecture can differ vastly from simple linear regression. For instance, the most powerful algorithm in supervised learning, on average, across a wide range of applications, is based on a collection (or a forest) of *trees*.[19] Trees, like in a decision tree, where the algorithm answers a series of questions sequentially to form an individual prediction. These different predictions are then combined to form a consensus prediction. How does that resemble linear regression? And there are tens of other architectures that are based on fundamentally different concepts.

The assumption of linearity is an interesting one too. It means that a set combination of factors (with set importance or weights) is sufficient to predict an outcome, with sufficiently accurate precision, over a wide range of output values. For instance, the same variables, with identical weights, should explain the credit score of a person, whether that individual is super prime or subprime. This appears to be a strong assumption. Also, linearity would imply that the outper-

19 For instance, for an extensive comparison of models over 165 classification tasks, see (Olson, et al. 2018)

formance of a given pair of stocks (one versus the other, as in statistical arbitrage) should always come from the same sensitivity to the same market factors.

Whenever we can hypothesise that there are various types of behaviours at play, likely, the relationship between input and output is not linear. The trouble is that we, humans, struggle with non-linearity. The simple fact that, say, data creation is growing at 50% a year[20] would render most of us unable to predict what that quantity means after ten years,[21] while we would have no problem understanding a linear progression. Also, coming back to the forest of trees, it would be impossible for the human mind to follow the algorithm's path. Linear regression is so much more comfortable. So, as much as we would like the world to be linear, it is mostly not.

MACHINE LEARNING IS GLORIFIED STATISTICS

Saying that "machine learning is a fancy word for statistics" definitely belongs in the top ten of AI platitudes. On the face of it, both statistics and machine learning could claim ownership of linear regression, for instance. They even use the same concepts, hidden under different names: *dependent* (or *response*) *variables* and *independent variables* for statistics, versus *labels* and *features* for machine learning. To add to the confusion, machine learning is sometimes called *statistical learning*, and both fields draw a lot from probability and mathematics. Finally, they both aim to make sense of data and solve problems through data analysis or inference.

However, without going into conceptual details, the two disciplines are fundamentally distinct in form and spirit. Machine learning ema-

---

20 Growth rates of the so-called *datasphere* vary significantly, but are undoubtedly high

21 That quantity would have grown by c. 58 times (1.5**10)

nated from computer science, while statistics is a sub-field of mathematics. This simple fact might offer the first clue. They have different objectives and techniques altogether. Statistics is concerned with representing data through *statistics* (like mean, variance, or higher *moments*), understanding relationships between variables, and inferring distributions and their parameters. Statistics uses a well-crafted arsenal of tools to ensure that data modelling is sound every step of the way. The central mechanism of statistics is hypothesis testing and the notion of statistical significance. Statistics builds model architectures that can be justified through parameter estimations, significance statistics (like *p-values*), and confidence intervals. Once the model is created, it could be used for predictions, but that is not the primary aim. Statistics does not venture into highly complex models either, because it could not *justify* them. As the guarantor of mathematical rigour, statistics must be able to justify and test its modelling choices.

Machine learning is the engineering parent of statistics. It mostly cares about results. This means being able to make accurate predictions (in a general sense) on unseen data. Machine learning attempts to learn directly from data without postulating hypotheses. Machine learning might build the same model – as in the case of linear regression – but the thought process is different. The model is deemed satisfactory if it generalises well, i.e. it performs well on new data (or *test set*). In statistics, there is no notion of test set per se: the model is suitable if it fits the data well, as measured by statistical metrics. As a consequence of its focus on performance, machine learning is freer to explore a much more extensive range of advanced models and architectures. Note that, in this process, it may lose explainability.

On a practical level, machine learning – versus statistics – does better at predictions, is usually more of a black box, involves more complex architectures, and handles higher dimensionality problems better. Also, foreign to statistics, machine learning is concerned with practical implementation and being production-ready. Modelling in machine learning is just a portion of the full *pipeline*, from data acquisition to producing live outputs.

Although statistics and machine learning may share the same high-level principles, they are in fact complementary disciplines. They might even be used together in a data science project. Statistics could take care of the initial exploratory data analysis (EDA) and possibly explain the *why*, while machine learning could throw all its weight behind achieving the highest possible predictive performance.

IN FINANCE, MACHINE LEARNING PREDICTIONS REPEAT THE PAST

A significant portion of datasets in finance involves time. They are not always expressed as time series, but there is a temporal element to them. Someone gathered data in the past in order to make live predictions in the future. As such, a natural criticism is that AI modelling can only predict what has been seen in the past.[22]

On some level, this is correct. Machine learning is not a crystal ball. It cannot anticipate what it has never been exposed to. By the way, it is easy to argue that this is true of human predictions as well. But, we need to dig a bit deeper into our understanding of that statement. Machine learning is about pattern recognition, but it is not simplistic pattern recognition. With the term *pattern recognition*, some might think that the machine matches the closest historical sequence to spit out as a prediction for the new sample of data it is forecasting. In other words, to predict the next day's performance, the algorithm could look at a similar sequence of, say, the past ten trading days, and predict that the output will be the same as what happened historically. That algo-

---

22 As in the compliance warning: "past performance is not a reliable indicator of future performance"

rithm is almost sure to generalise very poorly, and therefore would not be selected as a good model.

Fundamentally, well-trained algorithms – i.e. exhibiting good generalisation on unseen data – extract structure in the data. That is the learning mechanism, whereby higher-level concepts are inferred from the data. Akin to a child who does not need to be shown all instances of a ball to recognise one, the algorithm does not rely on mere rote learning.

Concerning investment strategies, even though the machine might not be able to predict the market with high accuracy, the process by which it builds a model is much more rigorous than what is currently being done in practice. I am referring here to the use of back-testing to devise trading strategies. It is almost certain that, after sufficient iterations of back-testing, an analyst will be able to build a strategy with as high a performance as he wants. One extreme approach is to learn the historical data entirely and predict what happened historically. Such a strategy has perfect accuracy on the data that it has been trained on. And, believe me, these so-called models are more common than you think in real-life. On the contrary, the machine learning approach has a well-established framework to maximise alpha discovery by minimising the overfitting risk.

Lastly, we need to be careful about what we mean by "present in the historical data". This has to do with causality. For instance, an episode of a pandemic might not be in the dataset. Therefore all attempts at predicting, through machine learning, the market reaction in such a situation are vain. Again, it depends. The pandemic might be the actual cause of an economic collapse, indeed. But, if markets do not trade on fundamentals, the absence of a pandemic episode in the past might not be that relevant. More pertinent might be that the algorithm has encountered countless occurrences of retail clients *buying the dip* in its training samples, and it will correctly extrapolate from such behaviour.

MACHINES MIMIC THE BRAIN

Deep learning (DL) is usually presented as computers replicating the human brain's operations. We have not come across deep learning much so far. The vast majority of today's machine learning problems handling large datasets are now solved through deep learning. Deep learning uses multiple layers to process input data sequentially to ultimately output a predicted label. The theory is that each layer learns a higher-level representation of the input as the signal progresses through the network.

As AI is ultimately interested in approaching (and surpassing) human intelligence, it is convenient to think that its most advanced architectures function like the human brain. And indeed, a particular form of networks, Convolutional Neural Networks (CNNs), that are highly effective at classifying images, are inspired by the way the visual cortex operates[23] in animals and humans. Also, as we saw earlier, the learning mechanisms in machine learning are similar to the ones we see in children.

However, it is epistemologically inaccurate to say that modern neural networks mimic the brain's architecture, as we still have limited knowledge of how the human brain functions. Neuroscience is a source of inspiration for AI architectures (and possibly the reverse, in terms of understanding of the brain), but this is more in relation to developing new ideas than replicating the brain's operating system per se. In summary, finance professionals may rest assured that we have not yet found a way to encode their thinking process.

23 (Hubel and Wiesel 1968)

4

THIS TIME, IT IS DIFFERENT

"Any existing structures and all the conditions of
doing business are always in a process of change.
Every situation is being upset before it has had time
to work itself out. Economic progress, in a capitalist
society, means turmoil."

Joseph Schumpeter

Over the years, there have been many false starts when it comes to
AI delivering on its promises. In the world of finance, expert systems were once omnipresent in financial planning, with large asset
managers and financial consultants placing high hopes on them.
The quant funds predicted that they would take over traditional
discretionary alpha generation but this has not happened yet either.
As with timing the market, it is not an easy task to embark on a
significant venture like embracing AI deep inside the organisation.
So, why now? Why take the plunge, or even pay attention? Because
at this very moment in time, there are powerful advance indicators
and specific developments in finance that are telling us that "this
time, it is different".

DATA + COMPUTATIONAL POWER

At a basic level, of course, the two driving forces of modern AI progress are the deluge of data and the ever-increasing growth of computational power. Without being too picky, they are both growing at around 40% CAGR, which is well into exponential territory. The rise of digital data and sensors alone should be enough to sustain that data expansion for many years to come. Without going into quantum computing[24] yet, Moore's law,[25] and the doubling of the number of transistors on an integrated circuit every one or two years, has been surprisingly accurate over the past 60 years. Other innovations like cloud computing or GPU/TPU[26] – useful for training neural networks – make practical AI a lot more of a reality.

On the AI side, some of the breakthroughs are only a few years old, particularly in the field of deep learning. Computers had reached superhuman levels in certain areas a long time ago, due to their memory and storage capabilities, like in processing a large corpus of texts or data. But, when the very same researchers who designed these new algorithms are astonished by their efficiency, I would argue that the whole community should pay attention.

IT WILL COME

Over the past decade, AI has taken other industries by storm, like healthcare, bioscience, and the automotive industry. But, nowhere is it more evident than within retail. These technologies have rede-

24 (It's official: Google has achieved quantum supremacy 2019)

25 (Moore 1965)

26 Graphics Processing Unit (GPU) and Tensor Processing Unit (TPU) are specialised processors used to improve performance

THIS TIME, IT IS DIFFERENT

signed entire business divisions. Which retailer does not dissect its consumers' behaviour for strategy, segmentation or advertising purposes today? Would you imagine understanding your consumer churn or your policy concerning client acquisition or retention without advanced analytics? Product and content recommenders are everywhere too. Of course, these clients leave a trove of digital impressions on social media platforms, retail websites, and tomorrow through Internet-of-Things (IoT) devices, but is the landscape that different for financial organisations?

Realistically, how likely is it that the same tools of predictive analytics will stop at the door of financial services? Data is ubiquitous in finance, between market data, economic data, business news, clients' data, etc. One can also argue that it is of a much richer nature than in retail given the variety of its sources, and therefore of higher value. I take the view that the primary reason why it has not progressed quicker compared to other industries is because of the complexity of the field. Modern finance has become incredibly intricate, and finance professionals are highly specialised. Problems are very different from one business area to another, and require domain expertise at every step of the way. However, as the tools mature and begin to be more accessible to all, and as technological knowledge becomes more widespread in the industry, it is only a question of time before the machines will rise.

Now, a more immediate question is when to innovate and which innovation to choose. The theory of innovation is complex – it involves endogenous factors of the firm, like the firm's position in the market, its size and resources. It is also about many other factors: knowledge spillover, uncertainty surrendering the innovation, ease of replication, etc. In that context, should you go for independent or cooperative innovation? Should you go for disruptive or incremental innovation? These are all valid questions at the firm's level, but, given

33

the competitive nature of the market and the overall social benefit, the answer is never to stay put.

Innovation in finance used to be about *financial engineering*. My bet is that *data engineering* – in the absence of a better term – will quickly rise to the level of the *financial engineering* that we have experienced in previous decades.[27]

IT IS COMING

The reality is that the trend has already started. Many surveys are already concluding that firms in financial services have embraced AI.[28] Of course, having just a handful of projects or business areas affected, at the level of a large company, still qualifies as early-stage, but it is in motion.

Other evidence of this trend is the explosion of alternative data.[29] I loosely define alternative data as data that is not usually collected, or that has not been historically considered as valuable data, or that is not traditionally used in a specific business context. Specialist alternative data platforms,[30] organising the purchase and sale of alternative datasets, have flourished. Even large banks[31] are now using their sell-side research to gather alternative data and promote it to their clients. Given the cost to providers, this is an explicit confirmation that a broader range of organisations is now looking for or consuming alternative data.

It is, therefore, safe to assume that some of your competition is already building capabilities in the AI field, even possibly in your

---

27 I do not take the simplistic view that financial engineering is a bad thing for society. It needs to be controlled and regulated, more than suppressed

28 (Bank of England; Financial Conduct Authority 2019)

29 See chapter 8 for further details

30 With companies such as: (Quandl Inc. 2020)

31 (Bank research embraces alternative data 2020)

business area. Also, we have seen that resource consumption, whether in the form of data production or computational power, is increasing at an exponential pace. Even if one believes that the pace of innovation is just accelerating, and maybe not growing exponentially, it is not a rational decision to be late in the race. The initial effort, in terms of resources and knowledge acquisition, will be increasingly difficult and costly.

ADAPT AND PLAN

Without scaring everyone with mentions of *workforce displacement*, the advent of such technology will undoubtedly have long-term effects. As a leader in an organisation, it is essential to understand the implications for your employees and the future fabric of the company.

On a positive note, this is a historic opportunity to shape the workforce of the future. New skills will be needed, new blood will join, and people will have to learn along the way. Without knowing what adopting such technology means and entails, it is difficult for a leader to adapt. Simple things like the introduction of the spreadsheet in offices in the early 1990s may give us an idea of what that looks like. Everyone has been using it on a day-to-day basis for decades now. The field of automated machine learning (AutoML), for instance, aims to democratise the tools of machine learning. In a not-too-distant future, it is very likely that simple platforms to perform standard machine learning tasks will be readily available. Online learning resources are already omnipresent as part of our training. New graduates now have to be able to code, in high-level languages like Python. As much as organisations have experienced massive productivity gains with office software, putting the tools of data analysis in the hands of everyone will be truly transformative.

UNDERSTANDING THE TECHNOLOGY

On that journey, and as a leader, it becomes crucial to understand what the technology can achieve. It is no longer sufficient to know that it exists. Computers have reached superhuman levels in some capacities but are still well behind human capabilities in others. For example, machines can ingest an entire corpus of business news produced since the dawn of time and figure out what each piece of news (or in aggregate) is about with an incredible level of insight. But, machines would not be able to summarise a business report, which an average student would be capable of. Unless you become familiar with the underpinning of the tools, that trend will increasingly become difficult to navigate.

On a side note, there might be another reason why you should care. Rightly so, there is a great emphasis on *conduct* and managing *conduct risk* within financial institutions. It has also become commonly accepted that *data privacy* and *data security* of your clients needs particular attention. I can predict that a fiduciary responsibility around data will also emerge in the years to come. To take a related example in market-making, it is no longer enough to get a price for an illiquid security from a couple of brokers to comply with *best execution*. There needs to be a more robust process around the use of data to justify compliance. In the future, your clients will expect that institutions base their decisions, for investment, risk management, product recommendation, etc., on extensive use of the data available. Making the best use of data will become one of your fiduciary responsibilities. And you guessed it, that will involve AI.

5

LOOKING UNDER THE HOOD: BASIC CONCEPTS

"1 + 1 = 2

The above proposition is occasionally useful."

Bertrand Russell

We will now take a deeper dive into AI, and its modern implementation technique, machine learning. Machine learning is a vast field that would require thousands of pages to cover extensively.[32] However, there are core principles that will go a long way in explaining the approach relevant to a large range of applications. Understanding these broad concepts will already provide a useful reading map for anyone looking to interact with machine learning engineers and query their modelling choices.

PROBLEMS MACHINE LEARNING CAN HANDLE

We have already come across the most common types of learning in machine learning: *supervised learning, unsupervised learning,* and *rein-*

---

32 There are additional recommended resources in the appendix for the interested reader

forcement learning. Reinforcement learning is the most recent of the three and looks incredibly promising (especially when coupled with deep learning) in some applications that resemble the most *general intelligence.* Reinforcement learning is a central component of the successes achieved in playing games (board games in particular), over the past decade. It involves the introduction of rewards to incentivise agents (players) to take actions within an environment. In particular, in a mechanism called *self-play,* the machine plays against itself, possibly millions of times, with the goal to earn the ultimate reward – a win. In doing so, the algorithm is able to self-improve over time. It has achieved superhuman performance even in the most challenging of all board games, the game of Go. However, reinforcement learning, despite its inherent elegance, does not yet have much concrete application in finance.

The most common technique in machine learning is supervised learning, which aims to predict a label when being presented with a new instance of data. More concretely and once trained, the model takes a set of inputs and produces an output either as discrete labels, in the case of a task called *classification,* or real-valued labels in a task called *regression.* Classes could be anything that takes discrete values, and the problem could have just two classes (*binary classification*) or many (*multiclass classification*). Classification tasks could be predicting whether a loan will default or not, whether the market will go up or not, the topic of a particular piece of news, a category for an unknown risk, etc. The poorly named *regression* is just the same task as classification, except that it outputs a continuous real value, like the price of a security, for instance. Quite often, these two types of tasks in supervised learning can be solved with the same algorithms, with one implementation for regression and one for classification.

On the other hand, unsupervised learning is a broader area in terms of the types of problems it can solve. There is no simple definition of unsupervised learning, except that it involves unlabelled data (i.e. in undirected tasks), and, broadly speaking, attempts to uncover structure or extract relationships in data. It can be used to make predictions or recommendations, for data exploration or data representation. Some of the main tasks are *clustering* (grouping of closely related instances), *anomaly detection* (the understanding of samples that differ substantially from the majority), *dimensionality reduction* (various tasks to reduce or project information onto a smaller number of dimensions or variables), *visualisation* and *mapping* of data (different tasks of plotting and representing high-dimensional data in a human-interpretable way).

PIPELINE: KEY INGREDIENTS IN A MACHINE LEARNING PROJECT

In 1997, Tom Mitchell gave a useful definition of machine learning: "A computer program is said to learn from experience E with respect to some class of tasks T and performance measure P if its performance at tasks in T, as measured by P, improves with experience E."[33] Let us unpack this definition, as it will help us understand the essential components of a project in machine learning. Here, we focus on the pure machine learning *pipeline*, which is the fancy name to describe the sequence of various data processing steps. Of course, in a real-world project, there are many other jobs – in an IT sense – that come before and after the machine learning pipeline: data acquisition, data storage and data transformation,[34] for instance, and later, model deployment, output publishing, system monitoring, system maintenance, model retraining, etc. We know by now what a task T is. It could be a particular classification task. Experience E covers the instances of data that we have access to. We will learn from that data. We need a measure of performance P to assess the

---

33 (T. M. Mitchell 1997)

34 Sometimes referred to as ETL, for *Extract, Transform and Load*

quality of the learning. The key in the definition is that, as we collect more data or experience E, the model improves its performance at solving the task. It is an iterative process that keeps learning (and adapting) over time as data is fed into the model.

So, to solve a machine learning problem, we start from a dataset that is fit for purpose, i.e. in a format that is understandable by the machine. For instance, it could be a matrix, stored in a file or database table, of rows, each representing an instance (sample), with features (variables) displayed across columns, and a label attached to every single row. We then need a model, which maps inputs (e.g. the features) to an output (e.g. a class). There is a range of possible models that define the algorithmic architecture to implement that transformation from input to output. A linear regression, which spits out a weighted average of the features as output, could be such a model – although this is unlikely in practice.

Then, an *objective function* needs to be chosen. Machine learning tasks are mostly represented as optimisation problems. The training of the model improves by optimising this objective function. For instance, if the objective function is the error rate between the predicted output and the true label (called *ground truth*), we want to minimise, through learning, that function and achieve as low an error rate as possible. Optionally, there is often a performance metric, which is not the same as the objective function, by which we ultimately compare the quality of the model, and possibly refine it. For instance, in a classification task, a typical performance metric is the *accuracy*, which measures the proportion of samples that are correctly classified (predicted class equal to true class).

In terms of processing, once we have chosen a model and an objective function, we split the data into a *train set* and a *test set*. The model is *trained* on the train set, which means that we run an optimisation algorithm of the objective function and update the

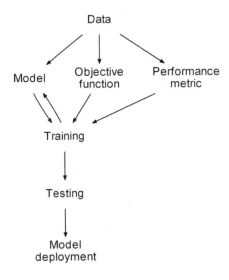

Figure 1 – typical machine learning pipeline

parameters iteratively until we are satisfied with the performance level. With these newly found model parameters, we can now make predictions on the test set – the portion of the initial dataset that was kept for testing. By comparing the predictions with the true labels, we can compute the performance metric on the test set and assess whether our model does a good job on unseen data.

MODELS THAT LEARN SOMETHING

A key consideration of machine learning is that we want the model to learn something from the data. We want the model to recognise patterns, figure out relationships between variables and extract structure from the data. After all, there is one way for a model to do perfectly, which is to remember every single label. For instance, if our model were to recall the performance of the stock market on every single trading day, it could perform perfectly on the data that it has been trained on. This is just rote learning and is not an intelligent learning mechanism (in the same way that a student who can only regurgitate lessons in an exam has learnt purely by rote).

This example is quite obvious and extreme, but this risk always exists in machine learning. It is called *overfitting*, which means that the model *learned* too much from the data, to the point of learning meaningless aspects, otherwise called *noise*. The gold standard in machine learning is to only test the performance of a model on unseen data, or test set. In doing so, we ensure that the model *generalises* well, i.e. that it has learnt enough of the structure in the training data to make meaningful predictions on unseen data. The model should have inferred just the right level of information from the data to be useful on new data.

Now, it is common in practice that the first attempt at modelling will not be the best production model. After all, there are many types of models, and also models usually come with *hyperparameters*. These are parameters that are not optimised by learning but chosen by the user. If you want to select the best model and associated hyperparameters, you would probably need to repeat the above process many times. Training the new model with its hyperparameter, then looking at performance on the test set, again and again. If you judged the performance of multiple models on the test set, intuitively, you learned something from the test set. You learned enough to compare models against one another. The test set is no longer *unseen data* as it has been used to discriminate between models.

So, now comes the platinum standard of model evaluation. The dataset is now split in three, a *train set* (to initially train the model), a *validation set* (to make all adjustments in terms of model and hyperparameter choices), and a *test set*, which is never used, until the model is in production.[35]

---

35 For further reading on an AI reproducibility issue, see (Hutson 2018)

OBJECTIVE FUNCTIONS

The field of optimisation, or the art of minimising or maximising[36] an objective function, is a vast subject in applied mathematics. In particular, certain functions are easier to optimise, from a computational standpoint. For instance, convex functions[37] are ideal candidates. Sometimes, this is just the practice of empirically experimenting with different functions over a range of problems that may favour one or another, the yardstick being the computational effort to reach the optimum.

In any case, for all practical purposes, it is sufficient to understand the two main functions used across many regression and classification problems. In regression tasks, the aim is to predict a real-value output as accurately as possible. By taking the average sum of the squared errors (the difference between predicted and actual labels) and root squaring it, one computes the *Root Mean Square Error* (RMSE), commonly used in regression tasks as the objective function to minimise. By taking the squared errors, the metric gives more weight to significant errors in the predictions. It is also convex, which is good for convergence.

For classification tasks, *cross-entropy*[38] – borrowed from information theory – is usually the measure of choice.

36 Note that taking the opposite of a function to maximise makes it a minimisation problem. In practice, objective functions are usually minimised, rather than maximised

37 A function is convex if the line segment between any two points on the graph of the function lies above the graph, like the squaring function

38 Cross-entropy penalises instances where the probability of belonging to the target class is low (through a logarithm) as an indicator of a wrong prediction

HOW DO MACHINES LEARN?

We have assumed a model, described by some initial parameters. We also have an objective function, calculated on some training data, that we would like to minimise. If we could find the optimal parameters of the model, for which the objective function is minimal, we would have built a model with optimal performance.[39] And this is how machines concretely learn. Learning, in AI, means finding an optimal set of parameters for our model, through an iterative process of optimisation. So, what is the workhorse of optimisation problems?

It is called *gradient descent*. It is even used in the most advanced applications of deep learning, where it is implemented in the famous *backpropagation*. To explain the principle of the solution, it is easier to visualise the function to optimise as a 3D shape. It looks like a mountainous region, covered in a thick fog. An agent is placed randomly on one of the slopes and is looking to go down into the valley, where the altitude (the function) is the lowest. Given the fog, it can only make small steps in a particular direction. The direction it chooses is the direction of steepest descent, as measured by the slopes around its current position. In repeating the process, it will certainly end up in the valley, and the function (altitude) would have been minimised. In mathematical terms, it is easy to describe the algorithm: gradient descent iteratively updates the function parameters by a quantity proportional to the opposite of the local gradient of that function, until convergence is reached (at a local minimum).[40] Rivers also find their path down to the valley in a

39 Obviously, on the basis that, for such class of models, and on that particular data, a good performance can be achieved

40 Gradient descent applies to differentiable functions, so that the gradient can be computed

Iterations in gradient descent algorithm

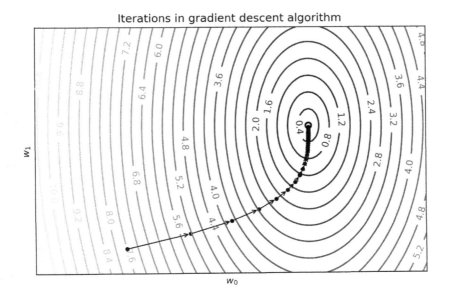

Figure 2 – illustration of the gradient descent algorithm. The arrows represent the steps of parameter updates, following the steepest descent down to a local minimum.

similar way. At each step, they follow the steepest line of descent to iteratively build the shortest path to the bottom of the mountain. The only difference, in the example of a river, is that gravity is the external force behind the solution and not some algorithm per se.

There are many variations to the underlying algorithm, for performance reasons or to deal with pathological functions, but the core principle is the same. It is satisfying to know that such a procedure is efficient in high dimensions too, and reassuring that it was invented by Augustin-Louis Cauchy in 1847.[41]

41 (Cauchy 1847)

PART TWO
AI IN ACTION

6

THE INDUSTRY FORCES BEHIND THE AI TRANSFORMATION IN FINANCE

"As for the future, your task is not to foresee it, but to enable it."

Antoine de Saint Exupéry

The financial industry – counting the banking system, asset and wealth management – is worth more than \$5 trillion in annual revenue.[42] This is a sector that *transforms* around \$260 trillion of funds.[43] Asset management alone, across retail and institutional, now manages close to \$100 trillion in Assets Under Management (AUM).

These numbers are staggering. They encompass a myriad of different businesses, with an incredible level of complexity and technicality. Few executives are now able to grasp all the activities within a large banking group. The business intricacies, regulation and risks are such that it requires a near-perfect organisation and informational flow to enable top management to take the appropriate decisions. In that context, how can such a profound transformation around AI even take place? Is it even appropriate to

42 (McKinsey & Company 2018)

43 Ibid.

attempt such a transformation? How can we prioritise where to focus our attention?

To answer these questions, it is useful to break down the industry into more manageable pieces. We keep hearing about *AI in financial services*, with vague examples around credit scoring, fraud detection, quantitative investing, etc. And, based on these simplified examples, anyone should be convinced about the potential of the technology. The only valid approach, to me, is to look at the prominent trends in the various sub-sectors, and see how precisely the technology fits in. It is important here to be as intellectually honest as possible. Are we addressing a large enough problem? Do we accurately know what we are solving for? Is the technology ready for it?

I would like to add one caveat to this. This bottom-up approach is too broad for day-to-day innovation. At the level of a business unit, and I will talk more about this later, the thought process is different. It is a combination of top-down and bottom-up approaches, but much more targeted at a particular function than at the broad level of the organisation. However, at an executive board level, thinking in terms of significant industry trends is helpful to start engaging in the transformation process.

Also, there is another pressing matter on the agenda. Financial services executives usually think in terms of peer competition. The quarterly benchmarking exercise across the industry naturally reinforces that trait. However, my view is that there might be a much more significant threat to the incumbents out there. *Fintech* could be one. But, Fintech has mostly moved from a position of *disruption* to one of *collaborative innovation*. Banks, in particular, have embraced this evolution. Sometimes banks are collaborating with Fintechs on developing internal solutions. Or, they are buying non-core services from vendors, in places where they might not have the required capex or expertise. In some cases, they are even happy with letting go of some parts of the value chain altogether. Banks have understood that – similarly to the automobile industry in the 1990s – many components in the banking process should be treated as *utilities*. From a shareholder standpoint, it only makes sense to compete in areas where there is a unique value proposition. So, Fintech is not the threat that we thought it would be a few years ago. Moreover, as a Fintech entrepreneur myself, I can assure you that the incumbents are capturing a disproportionate share of the value created by Fintech companies. It is incredibly unusual to see disruptors negotiating on a level-playing field with their large clients.

To me, the menace to traditional finance groups comes from much more powerful organisations. *Big Tech* has the means to compete and it has not just the financial resources, but part of the talent and expertise. Tech companies are already prominent in payments. They have also made forays into consumer finance, wealth and asset management. These are somewhat simpler areas, but also large revenue pools.

The lingering question is why this has not happened in a more meaningful way yet. Of course, regulation is a consideration. Financial services are, for the most part, highly regulated. It is much easier to make naive mistakes than to build trust with regulators. Also, up until recently, there was not much need for tech companies to diversify away from their core businesses – data collection and monetisation through ad selling. But, the landscape has changed. Their expertise in data and the network effect make them very credible players. The financial industry, as we have said, remains hugely complex, so it will take some time before we see meaningful changes. It is difficult to say when Big Tech will enter the race, but my bet is that they will.

That digression was meant to place the data and AI conversation in a broader context. As a senior executive, you probably do not want to wake up one day with a large tech company offering a superior product. And, I mean *superior* by several orders of magnitude. So, let us now start with our review of the industry landscape, and how recent trends fit with our AI discourse. It will be a broad-brush approach, with some selected examples. As previously said, reviewing every single opportunity would be impossible and counter-productive.

RETAIL BANKING: DIGITAL DATA AND OUTDATED SCORECARDS

Globally, retail banking has experienced a transformation on both sides of the balance-sheet, deposit-taking and lending, be it consumer finance or mortgages. Not dissimilarly to the rest of the retail sector, consumer behaviour and expectations have changed over the past decade and the digital segment has grown everywhere. Some emerging markets have even leapfrogged directly from an environment with minimal banking presence to full-blown mobile app banking. In traditional markets, banks used to grow as a result of expanding their physical presence. More branches meant more deposits and more products sold. Now, that correlation no longer holds. Across Europe and North America, branch closure is an ongoing theme. Still, the overall business has expanded through internet and mobile banking. More and more clients prefer banking online to having to visit their local branch.

The reality of modern retail banking is that clients are no longer attached to a bank's brand. They now have multiple accounts with multiple banks, shop around and value other things like the ease of use, the responsiveness, and the overall customer experience. It used to be easier to monetise the client wallet in the past, as loyalty was what enabled banks to cross-sell products. The plan was to attract deposits through branding or offers and extract value from the whole suite of products, from mortgages to loans, investments or insurance.

Now, due to regulation and better infrastructure pipes, having multiple banking relationships is much easier than before. Retail banking is more about experience and products, and it has become an innovative place again. After many decades of the same, we see neo-banks and Fintech players disrupting the landscape. They pick the low-hanging fruits, where they offer superior products and services using the latest technology.

There is another, quieter revolution that is also taking place and fuelling changes in the market structure. Since 2018, in the EU and the UK, and very likely in other regions soon, *open banking*[44] is pushing the use of *APIs* across financial institutions. APIs – *application programming interfaces* – are the technological solution to give third-party providers of financial services access to banks' data, down to individual transactions. Banks hold a precious asset, transaction data from their customers. Now, with the client's consent, that data can be made available to other companies. This is naturally a significant driver of innovation, as companies, not holding the relationship with a client yet, can now compete. This trend is related to other major consumer developments, like data ownership and *open data*, so it is likely to gain momentum.

In terms of financial performance, retail banks are plagued by low net interest margins (NIM). On deposits, the floor at 0% on rates is biting in Europe, as it is nearly impossible to charge retail clients for holding cash. But even, elsewhere, the deposit margin is constrained by the overall low level of rates. On the asset side, in many markets, the competition is fierce for asset deployment, in mortgages in particular. Given the limited ability to impact NIM through increasing margins, it is likely, for the foreseeable future, that the best course of action will be to focus on costs and increasing wallet share – through smarter client acquisition and retention.

44 Enacted by the Revised Payment Services Directive, or PSD2, in the EU

Given the profound change in the industry, the opportunities are multiple. Beyond the obvious digital transformation, and creating services to compete – or partner-up – with Fintechs, two areas are of particular interest. With increased digital interaction, clients leave a much wider footprint in banks' systems. To better understand clients' behaviour and interests, it used to be necessary to survey them or assess the success of marketing campaigns. Now, you can read these from their digital actions. For those customers from whom you can mine this data, it is of high value and quality. There is no longer any second-guessing and A/B testing[45] is not needed. The clients' actions speak for themselves.

This digital data is not to be confused with bank account data, which is, in itself, vastly underexploited. Understanding spending patterns and sometimes revenues at a deep level is crucial to forming a better idea of affordability and credit quality, and also to appreciating the microeconomic drivers through cycles. Across their digital and account footprints, clients leave a valuable source of data that can be exploited through new services, new products, and high-quality data-driven recommendations for products and services. For instance, tracking the dynamics of cash, at an individual level, can lead to innovative cash management products, for the benefit of the client and the bank.

On the lending side, what sets retail lending apart is its small size tickets and relative pool homogeneity. It is a natural place for machine learning, where systems can be fed with relevant, granular, live data. Exploiting bank account data, and other alternative data, is the next breakthrough, to create a high-quality credit scoring. We are all mindful that it comes with challenges – and

45 A/B testing is a controlled experiment where one measures the client's response to two versions, version A and version B, of the same product (for instance, two versions of the same website)

regulatory scrutiny – around fair lending, managing biases, and AI explainability. Nevertheless, this is an opportunity to increase financial inclusion, as well as improving credit performance. This was the original vision of marketplace lenders, when they appeared as competitors to bank lending, after the financial crisis. The dream has only been partially met, and banks also have an essential role to play. It is worth noting that the fee pool, across consumer finance and mortgages, is such that even small improvements in lending have a disproportionate effect on the bottom line.

CORPORATE BANKING: CROSS-SELLING

Corporate banking has been a slightly brighter spot within over-all banking, with more acceptable ROEs post-crisis. NIM has been good in North America, but still challenging elsewhere. The cheap-est source of funding, deposits, has become more competitive. When it comes to corporate lending, this is a tale of three tiers. Larger corporate clients are spoiled for choice, with multiple lenders and access to capital markets at historically low levels of rates. The second tier is also vibrant, with an incredible expansion of private debt outside banking. Large credit funds and institutional accounts engage in direct lending to an unprecedented level. On the contrary, SME clients find access to credit hard due to capital and operational costs faced by traditional banks.

So, in this world of constrained balance-sheets, competing on volumes is not the solution. What corporate clients value more in a bank, beyond pricing, is the depth of the relationship. They expect business partners to have in-depth industry knowledge. The products might be commoditised, but the service should not be. A new entrant will not be able to manufacture that depth from the start. Value-added services exploiting deeper client understanding have a long way to go. Also, for most segments, the credit offering is competitive, so cross-selling is the route to higher returns. It sounds like a cliché, but selling the whole bank, be it treasury products or advisory services, is more relevant than ever to this segment.

In that context, opportunities are plenty. Being closer to one's client can be supported by value-added services, like client relevant content, bespoke product recommendations though client clustering, or individual product pricing. All of this can only be supported by smart data analytics. This is the land of clustering, recommenders and natural language processing (NLP), or in other words, extracting structure from troves of data. The relevant data sources are CRM systems, transaction data, other client relevant data, industry and business news, market and economic data. NLP can be put to use as a source of more relevant conversations with clients or to generate leads at the banker or client level. It is already utilised to facilitate lawyers' work to prepare termsheets and contracts, review and search documentation databases. More obscure areas, like foreign exchange hedging or even cash management, can be supported with better advisory analytics as well. Also, with increased process digitalisation, more data will be available for better client servicing and prioritisation.

On the credit side, machine learning can help towards achieving automated pricing of smaller loans, which is a drag on opex. Especially in emerging markets with no credit scoring agencies, building or owning repositories of financial and non-financial data for SMEs is crucial before extending credit in these segments. Even for larger loan sizes, web crawling or analysing consumer touchpoints, in particular through social media, can assist with credit assessment to offer a more recent picture of financial performance. Similar tools, based on non-financial data, may also be used to detect early signals of credit or industry deterioration.

INVESTMENT BANKING: CYBORG BANKERS

Investment bank businesses have produced subpar ROEs after the global financial crisis, at less than half of what they were pre-crisis. This is particularly true in Europe, where the macro-environment is even more challenging, and the market much more fragmented, with no real pan-European player. Overall, sustained low rates and slow global growth have not been supportive of higher returns. Low ROEs have been driven by an inflated denominator, due to new regulation – especially around market and counterparty risks. However, to restore ROE, higher revenues or lower costs have not been achieved by any investment bank. The cost-income ratio for large investment banks consistently hovers around 75%.

As a result of bank retrenching, due to higher capital costs or a refocus on the core, the model of the universal investment bank – being everything to all clients – is dead. Banks have been engaged in a combination of reduced global footprint, reduced product mix and reduced number of clients.[46] At best, less profitable, i.e. smaller, clients were moved to a *low-touch* category, with access limited to electronic platforms. For global markets, such banks' retrenching has caused lower liquidity in many products. Banks can now mobilise much smaller balance-sheets, and competition suffers. Other problems are obsolete IT systems, which consume most of the funding towards technology. Innovating in that context is challenging. The cost of regulation does not seem to abate either.

However, despite this challenging environment for banks' boards to navigate, there are brighter spots. Like elsewhere in the industry, acknowledging that you do not need to own the whole value-chain has been a trend. Unbundling of services has started, especially

---

46 Still, some banks have managed to become product or regional champions

within the back- to middle-office, considered more and more like utilities. Specialist vendors can offer superior solutions at a lower cost. Also, Fintech cooperation can be an opportunity to move forward in areas where there is no unique value proposition. Global markets may become a place where talent and creativity are at the core of the value again, as opposed to taking unrestrained market risk.

From the investment bank of the future, unable to take on unlimited risk, clients will expect a higher quality of service. Sales will need to be *augmented* through smart systems. Mining an ever-increasing volume of structured and unstructured data, about clients, activity, markets, and beyond, the challenge will be to create actionable insights. Soon, a typical *cyborg* salesperson will be able to start the day with a condensed view of the recent market and business developments, especially when unusual activity has been signalled. She will know which clients to prioritise and what recommendations to make, in light of their positioning and the market developments. Particular trade ideas will be flagged to specific clients. Before taking on a transaction, she will know how to offload or distribute the risk. She will also be in charge of selling data packages tailored to the client's needs, based on the bank's internal content and third-party sources. She will become the pilot tuning the machine, but the machine could also fly solo in most conditions.

The trader, too, will be able to identify market regimes, to adjust his trading activity. As a market maker, he will benefit from automated pricing, based on a vast set of market data, encompassing prices, market activity and news. When not fine-tuning quotes for clients, traders will work on their trading signal system, automatically tagging any valid trading opportunity. Or, they could be adjusting their quantitative investment strategies or execution algorithms, tweaking parameters, models or inputs. Outside trading hours, traders will be reviewing and testing the new alternative datasets produced by the research department.

All this will be run with the bank's machines identifying early signs of system breakdowns, unusual risks, or making sure that the market operates as intended. This will automatically feed into regulators for market surveillance purposes. In the investment bank of the future, traditional financial engineering might be less prevalent, but creativity and ingenuity will undoubtedly be as widespread as at the best of times.

ASSET MANAGEMENT: TAKING ON THE INDEX FUNDS

The overwhelming trends in asset management have been a move towards passive investments and increased pressure on fees. Institutional investors have been shifting en masse to passive, particularly in the form of ETFs in North America. To complement their asset allocation, alternatives have steadily grown to provide the higher-yielding portion. In that reallocation, scale matters, with the more prominent brand names and players with an extended product range benefiting the most. Suffering the most have been actively managed equity managers. Generating consistent alpha has been an impossible task. Central banks' actions, higher asset correlation, and traditional factors being arbitraged away have been blamed for the lack of overperformance versus their benchmarks. Fees have been trending lower, in particular, due to regulation pushing for increased transparency, for instance through MiFID II in Europe. The move to index trackers and their relative performance has not helped either. A non-negligible portion of retail products has zero management fees.

Looking ahead, the market picture is not particularly rosy, either. Low yields have followed an incredible bull run in fixed income.

Many sovereign and higher credit bonds carry a negative yield in Europe. Growth prospects are limited, and asset prices are elevated. Operating costs are high, partly because of increased regulation and its cost of implementation. All this makes a bleak picture, with asset managers trading at low P/E.

However, these trends may also tell us a different story. It is time for reinvention and innovation. In a data-dominated world, asset management has been slow to respond, even though opportunities are everywhere along the value chain. Asset management has been mostly driven by products, access products that provide exposure to a particular corner of the market, rather than client services which have remained mostly untapped. It is time to move from products to client services and solutions. Clients have different needs, and these value-added services can be outsourced to asset managers. It makes sense because asset managers can support their decisions with data, and they have a unique vantage point close to the markets.

Institutional clients need CIO and portfolio allocation services. Insurance companies, across their businesses, require better liability matching strategies. Pension funds require investment funds to address the retirement conundrum. Retail clients want more thematic investing, in line with their beliefs and views. Markets and the investment world are ever more complex to navigate, which further complicates the task. Asset managers will provide a credible alternative to these problems if they can prove that they have developed a systematic and fact-based approach. The arsenal of data and analytics will come in handy.

Even in the challenging area of alpha generation, what investors expect is a rigorous approach. In a data-driven world, a manager's intuition is no longer sufficient. We can expect a robust alpha testing methodology to avoid overfitting and false positives, and to help underpin a duly tested risk management approach and a methodology for position sizing and asset allocation. We also hope that managers will relentlessly look for value in alternative datasets, to provide new trade signals and sources of alpha.

Execution has become more complicated, especially when dealing with reduced liquidity. It is no longer acceptable to just take the sell-side quotes. Machines can be trained to find the best options and data can feed price expectations. Computers are also good at combating human biases. They have many shortcomings, but they never fail and they never make mistakes. Biases in investment management are well documented. For instance, confirmation bias, where a manager sticks to her existing positions and changes the narrative to justify inaction.

So, if asset management embraces the data and analytics revolution, its future is exciting. Also – and this is something I touched upon earlier – I believe that a fiduciary responsibility towards investors around the best use of data will become a real thing. For instance, in private markets, it is not because data is not available or it is difficult to obtain, that, as a manager, you should not have a duty to gather as much insight as possible to support your decisions. Making a judgment call is reasonable if supported by tangible facts, or at least by an effort to find all relevant information.

WEALTH MANAGEMENT: CHANGING CLIENTS' BEHAVIOUR

Wealth management has experienced a similar trajectory to asset management. Increased fee transparency, a lack of product differentiation, and better performance of more established brands with scale have led to cost pressure. Other factors, specific to the industry, have also played out. Offshore centres have decreased in importance, because of the extensive exchange of tax information. Also, business performance is largely dependent on market performance.

Volatility is favourable for execution services, and markets trending higher for asset growth and, therefore, fees. Moreover, as in traditional banking, costs increase with lower rates, as deposit margin is reduced. Negative deposit rates, not charged to customers, has become a real issue in European private banking.

But, more fundamental is the change in some clients' behaviour, indicating possible further transformation of the industry. Younger clients, often identified as the millennials, have shown an appetite for alternative investment platforms rather than traditional wealth managers. Secondly, robo-advisory services have had relative success. Their offer is predicated on ease of use, sleek interface, simpler choices, and complexity hidden behind the scenes. It is largely about user experience. Lastly, China, which did not have much of a wealth management industry, for obvious reasons, has encountered noticeable changes. Technology platforms have been able to build an incredible user base in record time for newly created wealth services.[47] Surprisingly, this success was not due to higher financial sophistication among their users. Instead, it is entirely as a consequence of the familiarity of Chinese consumers with technology.[48] For the large wealth managers, in Europe and North America, these Chinese clients might seem distant. And, these millennials are irrelevant in terms of asset ownership at this stage of their life. However, this is a clear sign of impending behavioural changes.

In the meantime, it has become difficult to extract additional value from execution-only services – despite their attractive returns during market turmoil – given the competition offered by modern trading platforms. Private banks and other wealth outlets need to compete on the full suite of services. Like elsewhere, high-value

47 (Ant Financial extends dominance in Chinese online finance 2018)
48 (Why millennials are driving cashless revolution in China 2018)

content should be prioritised. For advisory, this means tailoring services to individual portfolios. Natural language processing can mine large bodies of news and market commentaries relevant to a particular client. Transaction recommenders are strategic too. Based on the client's existing exposure, relevant market developments, transactions done by other clients or relative value opportunities, machine learning can construct pertinent potential trades. These systems can be either utilised by the relationship manager or pushed to the end client. To retain clients, wealth managers should rather focus on quality of service and augmenting their salespeople. Too much effort is currently spent on just preserving assets, with lending and personal relationships the only tools to do so.

For discretionary mandates, the *best use of data* is to complement *best execution*. Clients have different objectives, and it is time to reinvent goal-based investing. The concept of personal balance-sheet, for instance, has been around for a long time, but current solutions are weak. Customers should expect a more comprehensive suite of solutions, genuinely targeting their aspirations. Data analytics is the product factory that can facilitate this. Automating investment is now easy, but the layer of smart portfolio allocation and CIO functions is still missing. It should not just be gimmicks exploiting trendy themes. A more robust approach addressing clients' goals and aspirations, risk tolerance, portfolio construction, execution and risk management is required. In this day and age, all these components can be tailored to the individual. It is also time for wealth managers to internalise more of the value creation. Otherwise, the trend of easy-to-use apps and passive investment portfolios will become the only answer.

PRIVATE EQUITY/VENTURE CAPITAL: A FRAGMENTED INVESTMENT WORLD

Private equity, and to a lesser extent venture capital, is predicated on in-depth industry knowledge, extensive due diligence, and a fair amount of financial engineering at closing. This is not a typical domain for machine learning engineers. Also, the industry has benefited from a shift towards private markets, as a complement to beta exposure in public markets. Partial isolation from market volatility, cheap financing, and maximised leverage levels have been reasons for its success. By definition, data is scarce in these markets, and sometimes quality is an issue. In particular, new businesses or those in transition are difficult to assess through data.

However, I see at least five clear opportunities to future proof their operations. Firstly, at a basic level, the industry is about making predictions about future performance. In particular, it is about identifying at inception which companies are more likely to lead to successful exits. One area of research is to identify drivers of favourable outcomes based on observed performance of similar companies. For early-stage companies, we tend to agree that the timing and the management team are two key differentiators. All these lead indicators now exist in databases. Team composition, profile of the founders, industry experience, competitive landscape, market environment, past funding rounds, and tens of other variables can be put to use to predict the probability of reaching the next milestone, whether it is a series A or an exit. To complement their intuition and reduce natural biases, the general partners can build shortlists of target companies, or size their investment according to the model.

Another promising area is in generating deal leads. The investment universe for venture capital and private equity is vast and typically unstructured. There are connections to be made between companies, to identify interesting vertical integration, supply chain or alternative opportunities to a potential investment. News and online data can already form a basis for such a network, through unsupervised learning techniques, and constitute a list of possible opportunities to track and conduct further due diligence.

Thirdly, the lack of relevant data might be an issue in the deal assessment phase. Also, financial performance is backward-looking. Beyond predictions about future performance – which in itself is more hazardous at company level – there is a more crucial need of *nowcasting*.[49] How can we assess the current performance – and possibly the very near future – beyond its past financials? Depending on the sector, there is a large body of data that can be extracted from digital footprints about the company's perception by its clients, its competition, etc. The exercise is costly, though, given the possibly numerous sources of data to collect, and, therefore, it only makes sense when conducting final due diligence.

Apart from deal leads and due diligence, data analysis can help tremendously in one of the core competency areas of private equity, operational efficiency of their portfolio companies. General partners bring industry and business experience, but this can be significantly augmented by data science projects. The idea is to push a clear agenda of data excellence within the portfolio companies. For maximum benefit, analytical expertise should be centralised at the private equity level. The fund's machine learning engineers can help build state-of-the-art models for their portfolio companies in areas such as marketing, sales, pricing, cost control or procurement. Rather than trying to assemble subpar teams in each portfolio company, it is more efficient to build a strong bench of experts to help the individual data

---

49 I loosely use the term *nowcasting* in this context, rather than in economics, to describe the forecasting of the *current* state of a company performance from other data sources

officers. Also, as an added benefit, the fund can use live data coming up from its companies for monitoring purposes.

Lastly, and particularly when more real-time data is available from their portfolio companies, data analysis can assist in identifying significant risk exposures. Equipped with such signals, general partners can take preventive actions accordingly. Such monitoring of the state of a company, industry or the economy can take inputs from many sources. But, at a basic level, building better capabilities for chief risk officers will become crucial for managing the fund through the cycle, and as a complement to good deal sourcing.

MARKET INFRASTRUCTURE: FROM RAW DATA TO DATA SOLUTIONS

Post-GFC, financial markets have transformed in a less visible way too. We tend to see the large players – banks, asset managers – but a profound shift has happened when it comes to the backbone of the market. Organised exchanges are well-known entities. But, over the past decade, a myriad of trading venues, execution services, securities services, clearing and settlement agents, technology, data and information companies have appeared to support the more visible side of the markets.

This has been an attractive domain for Fintech companies, founded by market specialists in the more technical areas of the business. Insider knowledge of what works, what could be improved or what could become a utility in the value chain is triggering genuine innovation. For the more mature companies, this is a high-profit-margin business supported by deep technological investments. Many companies in this sector operate at 40% or higher profit margins.

However, a shift is happening. As operators of the market, these participants process a tremendous number of transactions. These processes leave or create a vast footprint of digital data. Consequently, forward valuations of these actors reflect a premium for that propri-etary data. For instance, market data, pre-trade and post-trade, at exchange groups or trading venues have enormous intrinsic value. But, regulators are pushing for more data transparency, in initiatives like MiFID II. Initially, the shift was intended to help with market surveillance. But it is now more about creating a level-playing field with equal information (the open data trend) as well as complement-ing the move towards increased electronification of markets. With more market transparency, the value embedded in raw data reduces.

Therefore, the next opportunity for these operators is to further monetise their data assets. If the first-level data is more freely avail-able, it becomes necessary to extract value from less visible parts of the data. A concrete example is the centralised order book data. The regulation requires basic pre-trade data to be made available, and it is difficult to conceive of a state where all of the data would be pub-lished. That would be undesirable for normal market functioning.[50] Also, for most market participants, this is of little use. Nevertheless, there is a range of traders who value such more refined data. Things like market depth, market imbalance, dynamics of volumes, quotes and prices are all beneficial for traders and market-makers operating at higher frequencies. For low-frequency institutions, understanding execution risk over longer periods, like around market or economic data publications, or at different times of day, would also be useful.

The challenge – and the opportunity – for market infrastructure companies is, therefore, to package their proprietary data into a high-value differentiated offering for a range of participants. Proper seg-mentation of clients and their interests is necessary. These data solu-tions require extended data modelling capabilities and could include external (alternative) data sources too. Furthermore, some of these

---

50 Note that it would be in itself a technical challenge too, given the sheer size of it

datasets can qualify as truly *big data*, which conditions the type of processing approach needed. These computing capabilities are best centralised within a handful of actors.

Besides, these data packages can be further extended. Historically, buy-side clients and other market participants performed their market data analysis in-house. Execution facilities could take ownership of some of these initiatives, for the benefit of the trading community. For instance, improved execution protocols, trade cost analysis, security pricing, liquidity tools can all be handled by the vendors, as opposed to the end client. These are highly quantitative fields where operators can further monetise the value of the data they produce.

INSURANCE: EMBRACING THE SENSOR REVOLUTION

Within the insurance sector, I will leave aside life insurance – which is closer to asset management in terms of its data use. Data could indeed benefit all aspects of investment, whether it is asset allocation or liability-driven investment. Also, on the liability side, actuaries are accustomed to quantitative techniques to assess risk, so there is a natural extension to machine learning around capturing non-linearity and dealing with higher dimensionality.

It is in non-life insurance, despite being a rather conservative business, that a significant revolution is taking place. I am not talking about Insurtech. Most Insurtech companies, as within Fintech, are collaborating with the established players, rather than disrupting them. Streamlining internal processes with better technology or improving insurance distribution is indeed a more natural place for them.

The quiet revolution I have in mind is more ingrained in our daily lives. The rise of IoT and sensors, coupled with connectivity through 5G networks, will transform the traditional insurance industry, particularly for risk underwriting.

Sensors provide an avalanche of data points that can be embedded in the underwriting process. Traditional underwriting relies on broad risk classifications, with risk pooling being the mechanism of risk sharing among policyholders. With individual sensors, we are moving towards personalised insurance pricing. This is a fundamental change. Premiums are now expected to reflect personal behaviours and attitudes towards risk, as opposed to being driven by a statistical measurement of claims. The goal is to derive claim probability and severity from scores of data points, which by definition requires advanced modelling. Telematics devices in motor insurance are already an early example of this evolution. It is not fully personalised yet, but it helps with risk categorisation and ongoing monitoring. All other insurance sectors – health insurance, for instance, but business risk insurance too – will benefit from the widespread use of cheap sensors for underwriting.

The pursued benefits of sensors are superior pricing overall, as better data should reduce uncertainty and asymmetry of information, a quicker turnaround and a reduced underwriting cost. However, this novel underwriting comes with challenges. The well-known issues in machine learning-based credit underwriting apply here too. In particular, fairness and non-discrimination are potential issues, for which regulators will want to see robust control mechanisms.

Another established area of data analytics is insurance fraud. It is particularly prevalent in auto insurance, but also in the context of the misuse of medical insurance. For instance, analysing textual data in filings of insurance claims is a promising avenue for research. The arsenal of anomaly detection in machine learning, and its ability to detect rare occurring events, is also an area of continued research. Lastly, marketing and customer services are domains where AI can help, for example, to retain clients or mine data to recommend insurance coverage.

7

SELECTED USE CASES
IN FINANCE

"The mathematical expectation of the speculator is zero."

Louis Bachelier

Possible use cases are ubiquitous and abundant in finance: in trading strategies, algorithmic trading, market-making, risk assessment, risk management, fraud prevention, compliance and regulation, client clustering, understanding of clients' behaviours, investment advice, trade recommendations, asset allocation, mining textual data for insight, and so many more.

Like with any other scientific discipline, the limitations have more to do with our creativity, and our ability to frame the problem. On a concrete level, because resources are not limitless for any organisation, the challenge is to prioritise projects and to identify the low-hanging fruits, or rather to identify the projects with the highest impact from an ROI standpoint.

As a company takes stock of its data content, defines the most crucial business problems to solve, and translates these into questions that AI can answer, then naturally, the most promising use cases will emerge. Here, I will focus on a few concrete cases, using significantly different AI techniques, in various corners of the market, to evidence the line of reasoning. I hope that you, the reader, will find it useful in framing your concrete problems and to start thinking creatively about AI.

CREDIT UNDERWRITING

We start the journey with an example from the world of private credit. It could take place within a consumer lending institution, or within a credit asset manager willing to invest in credit assets. To simplify the presentation, we will take the point of view of a credit originator. Consumer finance – lending to individuals – has long used quantitative techniques to assess the creditworthiness of its potential borrowers. In mature credit markets, the approach relies primarily on credit scores, based on data gathered by credit bureaus. In the US, for instance, the FICO score[51] is used extensively for credit underwriting by banks and other lending institutions. Without going into the details of the scoring methodology, it applies fixed weights to relevant categories in the applicant's credit file: payment history (in particular credit incidents), debt burden (for instance, extent of leverage), length of credit history, variety of credit used (different types of credit are viewed favourably), and recent inquiries to the bureaus (too many inquiries for credit is a warning).

The shortcomings of such credit measurement have been discussed at length. Credit scores attempt to estimate both the *ability to pay* and the *propensity to pay*. This looks like a complex question, but credit agencies approach it in a very simplistic way. High credit scores are based solely on past behaviour. Take credit, repay

---

51 Input data to the credit score is from the three national credit bureaus: Experian, Equifax, and TransUnion

credit on time, and do it for many years, and you will be granted a high credit score. In other words, it has nothing to do with your particular situation or circumstance. It relies solely on the simple assumption that past behaviours repeat. If you repaid your debt in a timely manner in the past, it is likely that you will do so again in the future. Of course, I make it sound more preposterous than it is in reality. That correlation between past behaviour and current behaviour is probably quite accurate on large sample sizes. But at an individual level, it is undoubtedly too basic.

Also, there is an obvious question that comes to mind. What do you do at the start of the process? How can you even calculate a score? The answer is that the individual needs to ask for a small credit line at the beginning, and then move up from there. That naturally excludes many potential borrowers in the process, the young, those who have *thin credit files*, or the ones that have particular circumstances. For entire markets, like in most emerging markets, this approach is not even possible, given the lack of basic credit products, like credit cards. For credit inclusion, fairness,[52] and more broadly social good, it is certainly not satisfactory.

Fundamentally, in these days of data abundance, how can such a crude methodology still be the gold standard? This is where machine learning can help dramatically. If you are worried that pushing advanced modelling – and its associated resource requirements – to attain social good might not be enough to win the case internally, let me tell you about the business argument. Business objectives are about widening the net. It is lending to borrowers who do not have easy access to credit, and who are, by definition, less competitive than superprime clients. It is also about making credit pricing personalised

---

52 I thought for a long time that *fair* in "Fair Isaac Corporation" – or FICO – referred to *fairness*, but it is actually the name of one of the co-founders of the company

and more accurate, one of the key drivers of client retention. It also leads to lower delinquencies and defaults, due to more advanced credit modelling. It helps with navigating the credit cycle, as a better understanding of client risk profiles is needed to adjust origination to the macro-environment. It reduces opex and credit decision lead times because of the largely automated process. And regulators will thank you, because all the metrics you are targeting are conducive to a better functioning market, in terms of addressing the lending gap, fairness, client satisfaction, profitability, risk management and business resilience.

So, the solution is to feed machine learning models with individual loan application data in order to predict creditworthiness at an *individual level*. There are several options to specify the problem, but we will examine the option where we split our loan universe into two categories: the loans that ultimately repay, and the ones that default. This is a *binary classification* problem, within the realm of supervised learning. The aim is to teach the algorithm to correctly classify loans from a dataset of credits for which we know the performance outcome. Once we have trained our algorithm on a train set, we can test its performance on unseen data, or test set. In production, we can reuse the calibrated model to make predictions on new loans. These predictions will appear in the form of a probability of belonging to the *default* class – and by symmetry, the probability of belonging to the *performing* class. We can then map this *default* probability to a more business-like *credit intensity*, and use it for credit selection or pricing. On a regular basis, we can rerun the training part and include more recent data, which could reflect changes in credit conditions.

There are many modelling choices and subtleties that we have not mentioned here so as to focus on the essential aspects. Among these are the definition of the *default* class – do we look at default to term or before maturity to include more recent loans? Also, the mapping of machine learning-based class probabilities to credit intensities, the likely class imbalance (the repayment class is usually significantly predominant), the mechanism to go from default intensities to loan pricing or the issue of early prepayments.

Let us look at the key components of the project. Data, firstly, takes the form of a structured dataset where we have, for every loan, the loan and borrower attributes at the time of application as features, and the label, i.e. whether the loan performed or defaulted. The attributes come from three categories: loan characteristics, the credit file of the borrower, and additional alternative data. The credit file components are the same as the ones that would constitute a traditional credit score, and regroup all types of credits ever contracted (revolving or term loans, credit card debt, consumer loans, mortgages or other property loans, auto loans, student loans etc.), any delinquency or default, and current credit line capacity across existing credit accounts. Alternative data is everything else. It is not credit-related, and, most crucially, not taken into account by credit scoring agencies. These are things like a job description, employment history, income, homeownership, housing costs, history of other payments, like utilities, postcode, etc. Increasingly, it includes raw data about bank accounts, which gives an accurate picture of spending behaviour, discretionary versus non-discretionary, income stability, etc. Also, in markets with no credit files, or thin credit files, like in emerging markets, mobile phone usage data has been used with great success to predict debt repayment.[53]

Data enrichment may be used to include other variables not collected at the loan level. For example, postcodes – partial, for privacy

---

53 Other experiments have been run, for instance, on younger borrowers, with data downloaded from their smartphone, showing usage of phone and apps

reasons – can be mapped to public datasets, to extract things like average income, housing costs, unemployment, etc., at a local level. These provide a valuable further understanding of the borrower's profile or regional dynamics. Lastly, macro-economic data – whether absolute levels or trends – can be added to better assess the credit cycle and overall macro conditions. Beyond unemployment, these can include measures of growth, financial markets metrics, or the competitive landscape, like the typical price of consumer credit facilities or lenders' concentration.

On the modelling side, any classification algorithm may be a contender. In general, tree-based ensemble models, like Random Forest or Gradient Boosting,[54] are very capable of dealing, in particular, with overfitting. It is worth mentioning that feature engineering, to select features or to create richer ones, is a necessary first step, and usually involves domain experts. The primary reason why such sophisticated models work in practice is because they can effectively handle high dimensionality (many per-loan features) and non-linearity. Non-linearity in consumer lending is present everywhere, and would not be captured by linear models. This may be a complex subject in modelling, but its manifestation is simplistic. Variables do not have a constant importance across all loans – as would be the case in linear models. Income matters in the belly of the credit spectrum, but not that much for higher or lower credit. Homeownership may be a plus overall, but renters are better candidates when middle-aged as they might already be stretched with family commitments. Inquiries to the credit bureaus are irrelevant below a certain threshold but become a clear negative signal above an elevated level. The list goes on. Only non-linear models have a chance to capture these complex relationships.

54 See chapter 12 for further details about these models

Concerning performance measures, a *Receiving Operating Charac-teristic* (ROC) curve[55] is the most relevant first indicator. It computes pairs of *false positive rate / true positive rate*, depending on how selective we want to be with the higher risk loans. Ideally, we want as high a true positive rate (the proportion of bad loans correctly identified) and as low a false positive rate (the percentage of good loans classified as bad) as possible. With a ROC curve, it is easy to compare a given machine learning model to other models, and in particular to traditional credit scoring. In prime credit markets, it is common to see a machine learning-based credit score being at least twice as informative as a conventional credit score.[56] In other markets, credit scoring is usually of no use, and machine learning is the only way to assess creditworthiness. Another useful metric, closer to business needs, is to compute the default (or delinquency) frequencies for various quantiles of machine learning credit scores. There should be a high correlation between the credit score and the default rate. For investors in the asset class actively selecting loans, it is useful to quantify the *alpha* of the selection process. If the manager selects higher-quality loans, as perceived by its machine learning model, to what extent does that translate into a higher portfolio performance?

Machine learning-based credit scoring is highly efficient in consumer lending. Given the granularity of the business, this is an area where it is often possible to train models on millions of loans. Despite its good results, machine learning is not used at scale yet. One reason is regulation. Regulators want to make sure that it is not at odds with fairness in lending. Possible biases in the data and model explainability are the key issues. It is therefore absolutely necessary to have a robust development process, whereby tests are accurately documented,

---

55 See later sections in the book for further details about performance metrics

56 As measured by the distance to a random classifier (source: author)

particularly with respect to biases. AI explainability is still an area in development, but there are already sufficient tools to address this concern. I firmly believe that there is only one path ahead. Assuming that we have the appropriate safeguards, using these kinds of techniques is much fairer, and undoubtedly contributes to social good. This is why it is only a question of time before these underwriting models become commonplace. Regulators cannot impose extreme simplicity, as in current lending models relying on basic formulas, and expect a safe and fair market at the same time.

RECOMMENDER SYSTEMS

In a financial world where products are somehow commoditised, providing relevant content to clients becomes a differentiating factor, as well as a driver of business performance. Use cases in our daily lives for recommender systems do not need to be spelt out. They govern how we interact with pretty much everything digital. Netflix ran a famous experiment from 2006 to 2009. They offered a prize of $1,000,000 to the team who could improve their existing recommender system for movies by more than 10%.[57] Tens of thousands of teams entered the contest, and the prize was awarded in 2009.

In finance, applications are ubiquitous for recommending transactions or relevant content. For instance, it can be used to push sales or analyst commentaries, or pieces of news to clients, without them having expressed interest in it. The critical element in a recommender system, and why it is based on machine learning, is its ability to extract a higher-order structure – through unsupervised learning – to make an inference about a client's interest. Say, as a salesperson, you like a particular news story. You could try to extract the key themes in it,

---

57 As measured by the RMSE on a test set hidden to the competing teams

and, remembering which clients consumed what within your client base, you could propose it to them. You hope that, in providing them with relevant content, you may receive more business from them. The issue is that you can only read so many stories. Extracting topics, unless they are apparent and have been previously tagged for you, is tedious. You can only cover a minimal set of clients this way, and you cannot remember everything they ever read – even if you have access to that information. I am sure that some of you, maybe in sales functions, will argue that this is called *knowing your client*. I will not get into that argument. Recommender systems just do this far quicker and on a massive scale. More importantly, they are able to extract relationships that no human being could possibly identify.

A particularly compelling application of recommender systems is in illiquid securities trading, for instance corporate bonds. The primary issue for dealers these days is to hold as little an inventory as possible. Bond inventories are expensive from a capital and funding standpoint, and minimising them could be what makes the difference between a profitable market-making desk, and one that is not. For coverage people, recommending relevant securities to clients is undoubtedly useful in order to be positioned as their preferred counterparty. Corporate bonds are a suitable application for the technology, as both the number of securities and the number of entities involved in their trading are large.

Recommender systems fall into two camps, *content filtering* and *collaborative filtering*. Our pocket example regarding news topics previously was a content filtering approach. As its name indicates, it requires the knowledge of the features for the items to recommend. For bond recommendation, content filtering would need to have access to bond metadata, like currency, country, sector, seniority, rating, issuer, etc. By computing similarities between bonds, and by creating client profiles based on past interests, the software can make new bond recommendations. In some contexts, content filtering is desirable. However, for our use case, it has the limitation of only recommending bonds similar to what was of interest to a particular client before, without the ability to offer novel suggestions.

Collaborative filtering is much more powerful and is radically different. The particularity of collaborative filtering – hence the term *collaborative* – is its reliance on the behaviours of groups of agents to infer recommendations. In bond recommendation, it is based on the principle that various types of clients trade groups of securities differently. It is intuitive to accept that yield hogs might buy high-risk junk bonds, while life companies might prefer safer long-term bonds – and maybe some low investment grade at the short end – and so on. Traditional techniques might try to manually come up with these trading patterns and clusters of clients. Machine learning-based recommender systems aim to unearth this structure, automatically, from data only. Also, the input data is straightforward and is only constituted of interest or transaction logs, pairing bonds and client interest over a given period. For instance, RFQs[58] received by a dealer would be sufficient for this task.[59]

An interesting feature of collaborative filtering is that it is domain-agnostic. The machine does not know anything about the characteristics of the bonds or the clients. As long as there is a measure of interest – or a rating, explicit or implicit – for a pair bond-client, we can infer recommendations. Therefore, it is applicable in many settings. By contrast, in content filtering, there is the need to define relevant features for the bonds to rate. Also, the definition of the *similarity function* makes an implicit assumption about the relative importance of the various features and requires guidance from

58 Requests For Quote
59 The ability to see a larger set of RFQs is obviously helpful to make more educated recommendations

domain expertise. In simpler terms, collaborative filtering is a lot more autonomous.

One aspect worth mentioning is related to the nature of the input matrix, i.e. the set of RFQs. It is *sparse*, meaning that, for the vast majority, we do not know the interest of a client for a particular security. Most elements of the matrix are unknown and are the purpose of the analysis. And, the question we want to answer is: how much interest does a specific client have in a particular bond?

Once we have inferred these missing quantifications of interest, we can use them in two ways. For a particular bond, say that a market maker is holding on balance-sheet, the salesperson can rank the entire population of clients by their interest in the bond. This constitutes an ordered list of clients to contact, with the highest chance of offloading the bond to. Besides, if a specific client has made an inquiry for a given bond that the market maker cannot source, the ranking of bond interests for that client will enable the coverage person to offer alternatives.

We will touch on the algorithms that can be used for such a task. As the goal is to extract a latent structure around client groups and bonds, they revolve around dimensionality reduction. Latent Dirichlet Allocation (LDA), Non-Negative Matrix Factorisation (NMF) or Autoencoders[60] are all valid candidates. A typical first choice is NMF. We represent the initial RFQ matrix as the product of two low-rank (of smaller dimension) matrices. The training minimises the distance[61] between the known interests and the reconstructed ones – through matrix multiplication. The smaller dimension of the matrices expresses the fact that the information contained in the sparse interest matrix is smaller than assumed in the large initial matrix. That information

60 See chapter 13 for further details about these models
61 Usually the Frobenius norm

can be summarised in smaller representations, as per the two matrices. Actually, these two matrices have clear interpretations. One represents the *location of the clients*, and the other the *location of the bonds*. Similar rows in the first matrix show the proximity of clients, while related columns in the second matrix exhibit close bonds.[62]

Let us talk about performance metrics in this particular context. This time the training metric is not the same as the overall performance metric. The distance between the two matrices is indeed not particularly insightful for the business. A more common approach is to keep a hold-out set, or test set, and measure the quality of recommendation on that unseen data. We then vary the number of top (n) recommendations, say from 1 to 50, and we measure, for each expressed interest, the proportion of times the pair client-bond was correctly predicted within the top n recommendations. In production, we can keep monitoring that score to assess the performance of the recommender over time.

When judging a business solution, it is useful to compare it to simpler or existing alternatives. For this problem, it is undoubtedly insightful to recommend the top clients that previously inquired about a particular bond as contenders for the next RFQ. This *baseline* becomes the one to beat with our more sophisticated model. Usually, in bond recommenders, the NMF version tends to do similarly to the naive baseline of frequent traders of the bond, when n is low. Indeed, it is intuitive that, if we allow for one recommendation only (n=1), the most likely next trade will come from the client that traded that bond the most frequently. But, if we relax the number of top recommendations, we get better results from NMF. Beyond the top clients, the frequentist approach is too naive

---

62 I have assumed that clients are represented in rows, and bonds in columns, in
   the interest matrix

and does not express the richness in the data. NMF is able to make connections with other clients that traded similar bonds, which the naive approach just cannot do.

A related topic is the business benefit from such a model. The obvious benefits are to increase the hit ratio of the desk, boost balance-sheet velocity, decrease balance-sheet costs, reduce time spent by sales, and improve desk profitability. But, there is another aspect to recommenders. The richness of their recommendations makes it a valuable aid for coverage people to strengthen their relationship with their clients. More often than not, thanks to the quality of the advice, clients trade other bonds with the dealer, if not the one recommended. It is an additional metric that might be usefully included in the performance measure.

There are many technical aspects that I have chosen not to expand on. Very often, due to different levels of engagement from clients, it is necessary to normalise activity across clients. Otherwise, large clients will dwarf the analysis and make it challenging to produce more unusual recommendations. Also, I ignored the time element in the recommendations. It does not make much sense to train the model just once and use it for recommendations in a later period. Also, I did not comment on the choice of the rank of the matrices, or in simpler words, the number of clusters of clients (and bonds). This is a hyperparameter that typically needs to be tuned. Also, the period length to train the model needs to be chosen. How far back should we go?

But most importantly, in practice, it is necessary to build a set of models that capitalise on their strength to refine recommendations and to explore other dimensions in the data.[63] In particular, it is useful to use

---

63 One of the techniques is called an ensemble, or a collection of models that make individual predictions. However, I would not go as far as the winning team of the Netflix prize which used 400+ models to select from. See (The BellKor Solution to the Netflix Grand Prize 2009).

content filtering as a complement to collaborative filtering techniques. In summary, despite their caveats, collaborative filtering recommender systems offer incredible advantages. They are easy to implement, require very little data, and can be used for many types of content.

TOPIC MODELLING

The world of finance, and in particular within global markets, is dominated by text. However, most of the data that is being analysed is still mostly numerical. These are primarily data pieces that quantify the state of the economy or businesses, like economic data or company earnings. They are obviously informative, but they have the disadvantage of being infrequent, with monthly or quarterly releases. Also, markets function on a well-established mechanism of forecasts and analysts' estimates. Once the data piece is released, it is quickly incorporated in prices, depending on the degree of surprise to the upside or downside.

The effect of the quantitative data piece quickly evaporates. It is a sign that it is only a metric summarising much more complex phenomena. The rest of the signal is elsewhere, in the myriad of bits of information, news, company releases, commentaries, and market sentiment that are continuously disseminated. Also, this textual information might be more persistent through time, as the transmission mechanism into prices is more subtle. A 20% positive earning surprise is easier to trade than a company press release announcing significant capex spending. So, despite what the Efficient Market Hypothesis states, textual data requires analysis before it can be fully priced in, and that is precisely what makes it useful.

Irrespective of these arguments, nobody will dispute the information overload we face. How can we follow so many moving parts, across markets, countries, sectors, even outside business and economics? We have established that human language remains a complex area for computers to master, given its subtlety. However, machines are superhuman when it comes to processing vast bodies of information.

It is an area where the association between human and machine is especially complementary. Imagine a world where you could retrieve a precise piece of information in a particular area of interest. Or, where you could understand what the key themes are in thousands of documents, without ever reading them. Or, understand what a foreign market is currently talking about, without having any connection there. Or, figure out what drives the investment community, how things are changing over time, and if there are emerging themes worth following. Or, being informed in real-time about a possible market-moving piece of content on Twitter, in an area you follow.

The field of topic modelling is doing just that. It takes as input a *corpus* of documents and can infer *latent* topics present in the corpus, without being guided. We covered one popular approach in a previous section, about dimensionality reduction. Latent Dirichlet Allocation (LDA) is another approach – probabilistic – that represents documents as a mixture of topics, which are themselves associated with a collection of words. The *model inference* is able to retrieve these topics automatically. These topics can usually be interpreted by the user on the basis of the (weighted) collection of words that constitute them. If we have "US", "Donald Trump", "China", "tariffs", "trade wars", it is easy to label the topic.

Once topics have been extracted, one can exhibit the essential documents related to a topic, classify documents, extract relevant content, get a picture of the relative importance of topics across the corpus, follow their influence over time, etc. The technique is extremely powerful in assisting human judgment and is typically something that humans would not have the capability to do.

There are many variations of the approach that can take into account things like sentiment or stance, for example, in corporate press releases. But already, in its basic form, it can be immensely useful to financial professionals to create client and deal leads, to be alerted about interesting pieces of information, or to follow a broad range of markets. In these, I find two applications particularly useful. The first one is about following topics over time. The latent representation of a corpus of news can be seen as the essence of what moves a market. For business and financial news, these topics are, at a given point in time, what feeds the market participant community. At an aggregate level, there is nothing else. Knowing this can be tremendously useful. For instance, it can help investment specialists in a corner of the market follow whether a particular set of news has filtered through the market, giving positioning opportunities. Diversity of topics can be informative too. A more concentrated market in terms of drivers is usually associated with market volatility. The prevalence of some themes can also be associated with a particular direction of the market.

Another domain where topic modelling can be advantageous to its users is when tracking multiple markets at once. Notably, in foreign language markets, it can be almost impossible to follow what the local market participants react to. As a foreign trader, you are at a significant disadvantage. You are dependent on the information feeding to your brokers. But how likely is it that they have a global and impartial view of the market? Is it an obscure election dominating the market talk, is it an incoming pension reform, is it something else? Topic modelling, especially in its trended version, can offer a real-time condensed version of a market. It can also scale easily to any source of data.

Like before, I have omitted some subtleties of the technique to focus on its use cases. In particular, I would like to mention the issue of labelling topics – which the machine cannot do. There are techniques for both supervised and knowledge-based approaches. In finance, though, the vocabulary is specialised and precise enough to make it less of a concern to the user. Also, the choice of the number of topics is addressed through the usual methods of algorithm performance. In the context of topic modelling, performance is typically assessed by computing metrics of topic coherence on a hold-out set. If a new, unseen document is evaluated by the model, a document being a mixture of topics themselves being distributions of words, how good is its composition of words versus what the model expected?

Rather than being a specific use case, topic modelling is an effective technique in a variety of tasks. It can extract meaning, thanks to natural language processing, that is best used as an aid to the human for insight or to guide decisions.

ALPHA GENERATION

Let us start with a story that some of us might have come across, maybe not in these exact terms, but in spirit. Let us imagine an analyst, who has noticed, over the recent past, that stocks that got hit the hardest tended to exhibit a follow-on reversal. In reading the literature about it, there seems to be evidence that day session declines might be followed by night reversals. The first model that the analyst builds estimates the night reversal based on the day's decline. There is no consistent performance. Then, she splits the dataset into deciles of daily performance and only goes long the first deciles – the weakest performers. She attributes this effect to some sort of a market overreaction. To exploit that idea further and be market neutral, she decides to go short the top deciles too. The performance seems promising in terms of Sharpe ratio. Then, moving from midpoints, she decides to test the algorithm on real brokers' quotes. Suddenly, the performance drops. Thinking it could be due to the bid-ask bounce and poor liquidity, she chooses to eliminate stocks trading below a certain threshold to avoid too wide bid/offers and high transaction costs. It improves, but not sufficiently yet. Then, she thinks it could be due to the universe being too broad. Maybe, only selecting volatile stocks, over longer periods, might be helpful, as overreaction might be more pronounced for them. Or, perhaps looking at stocks that were not on a long-term decline, to just focus on sudden shocks. Or possibly, choosing a better intraday execution, away from market open, when liquidity is reduced. Or changing the observation period, as the market microstructure has evolved from ten years ago. Etc, etc.

I am sure you get the idea. After sufficient iterations and tens of backtesting, the chances of finding *alpha* are very high. The problem is that it is also highly likely that what has been modelled is the noise itself, and not the signal in the data. Repeated backtesting to identify alpha carries a high risk of overfitting. Even if a hold-out set is kept, the model and parameter changes over time will subtly push towards overfitting on even the test set.

Machine learning is not a silver bullet for alpha generation. But what it offers is a data analysis framework to handle hypothesis testing in a robust framework. Overfitting is primarily observed on the train set and can be addressed with keeping a tab on generalisation error. As we will see later in the book, the key is the use of cross-validation, model regularisation, and the reduction of variance through ensemble models. To address test set overfitting, it is good practice to keep a validation set for hyperparameter tuning, to make sure that experiments run many times do not learn the test set structure. Ideally, it is best if more data can be collected, or maybe the model tested on related markets. In currency or single stock markets, for instance, this may be a feasible option. Soon, thanks to deep learning, we will certainly be able to generate synthetic datasets[64] that have the same statistical properties as the historical path. Text and music sequences are already credible enough. It is only a question of time before the same applies to time series modelling.

64 Through architectures like GANs

8

(ALTERNATIVE-)DATA, ANYONE?

> "What information consumes is rather obvious: it consumes the attention of its recipients. Hence a wealth of information creates a poverty of attention, and a need to allocate that attention efficiently among the overabundance of information sources that might consume it."
>
> Herbert Simon

In Ancient Babylon and for hundreds of years, scribes meticulously wrote the prices of six commodities on clay tablets.[65] It is now accepted that these were market prices, reflecting demand and supply forces, even sometimes showing signs of intense volatility and frequent repricing. But even more interestingly, these tablets also contained measurements of water level changes of the Euphrates River. It is unclear whether these recordings were an attempt to predict prices, based on the quality of the crop to come. But, the close proximity of the two sets of data is intriguing.

More recently, it has been possible to analyse flight data for an unusual purpose. Combining ATC data – which records in real-time communications with aircrafts – with various databases of

---

65 (Temin 2002)

plane registrations and airports, one can reconstruct the flight paths of corporate jets.[66] The destination and frequency of these trips have been proven as valuable inputs in predicting M&A activity. Knowing that senior management have visited certain places regularly may be invaluable for investment professionals in their assessment of upcoming deals. Not long ago, you could only do this if you had people on the ground at various airports, and the whole operation would be complex, costly and tedious.

Since time immemorial, investors and traders have tried to find an informational advantage to predict the direction of market prices. This is not specific to the current data and technological revolution. However, what has changed is that these attempts have become much more widespread and commoditised. With data now being systematically recorded, the ease of access has dramatically increased. The collection of data is greatly simplified and does not require sending people to record it physically. Also, its dissemination is facilitated, with platforms and vendors providing access to databases through modern technologies like APIs, possibly in real-time.

The alternative data – or alt-data – revolution is well underway.

TYPES OF DATA IN FINANCE

However, let us take a look at the types of data that are typically, and still primarily, used in finance to forecast markets. Firstly, a whole range of asset prices, recorded at various frequencies (up to tick data) and levels of depth (up to a full order book). These are used to assess things like correlations and auto-correlations in order to find causality in market developments.

---

66 (Strohmeier, et al. 2018)

Then, global markets are punctuated by the release of economic data, to understand the broader state of the economy, at a worldwide, regional or industry level. These are regularly produced – with significant time lags – by government agencies and supranational bodies, alongside sets of sell-side analysts' forecasts.

At a company level, and particularly for quoted companies, investment professionals have access to quarterly financial statements, regulatory filings, press releases, and a myriad of analysts' reports and earnings estimates. Finally, less specific and less structured, industry, business, political and general news complete the landscape.

In this context, alternative data – loosely defined as what is not traditionally used in the investment process – initially emerged to address two primary issues. One is the information edge. As information systems progressed, most of the standard data became more readily accessible to more market participants, and beating the markets became increasingly difficult. Preserving an informational advantage is now about moving to less accessible – and maybe less interpretable – data. The other driver is about immediacy. Market releases are typically low-frequency, and, in between publications, it becomes necessary to access higher-frequency – but related – data.

THE STORY OF THE MODERN EQUITY ANALYST

If traditional data is no longer sufficient, what else could provide an edge? For this, let us turn to an equity analyst with unlimited access to alt-data and a willingness to get an in-depth view about a specific company. The analyst is covering a retail company with multiple consumer sites.

Firstly, the analyst could request access to satellite data to measure the numbers of consumers' cars and suppliers' trucks on the company's parking lots to assess business activity. Inside or around the retail stores, geolocation data – through mobile, wifi, bluetooth tracking or QR codes scanning – would also be a good indication of foot traffic.

Online, product price tracking – and possibly of competitors' products too – on aggregator websites would help form a view of the price dynamic, supply forces and competitive landscape. Comments about the brand on social platforms, coupled with a sentiment analyser, would reveal customers' perception. Attention to complaints and their handling would also be useful to better assess client satisfaction. Product reviews on specialist websites could be instructive for product quality and customer fit.

Concerning corporate strategy, Google queries could be a good source of customers' trends and the overall demand side. Web scraping of influential bloggers could complement the analysis.

At the company level, news stories about the company in various media could reveal potential issues. Web scraping of job boards would enable the analyst to confirm areas of investment where new hires go. Insider trading records could assist with the stock price expectation from the inside. Of course, government agencies' datasets – which are growing in number every day in the *open data* world – could add more specific information, like patent filings, where relevant.

During earnings calls, an analysis of vocal emotions[67] of senior management would facilitate the reading of the company's future performance, as perceived by the leadership team. Even measuring the facial width-to-height ratio of the CEO, as a proxy for testosterone levels, could be an input correlated with the risk of misreporting.[68]

I will finish with a word of caution for the analyst. If his picture is on LinkedIn, he might, in turn, be assessed for "approachability,

67 (Mayew and Venkatachalam 2012)
68 (Jia, Van Lent and Zeng 2014)

attractiveness, and dominance", which may affect the perception of the report quality.[69]

ALTERNATIVE DATA ECOSYSTEM

What we have seen through our imaginary story is how pervasive alt-data is. From virtually none ten years ago, there are now more than a thousand alternative data providers. Even sell-side research is blending alt-data with their traditional research to provide their clients with augmented insight.

Companies like Quandl[70] operate data aggregators to provide a vast range of alt-data sources to investment firms. Interestingly, these operators are also buying datasets from individual businesses that may collect data as a by-product of their operations. For instance, a credit card company may license quasi-real-time anonymised data about the transactions they process.

The types of data these alt-data companies sell are difficult to characterise. If you think about it, the possible data uses are only limited by our imagination. Unexpected sources of data may prove useful in certain circumstances. For instance, an online company offering measures of wifi bandwidth to individuals could suddenly find its data helpful in an unsuspected way. The aggregated data could help measure the extent of "work-from-home" and the business disruption during a pandemic.

The most sophisticated hedge funds may have dedicated employees whose role is to buy untapped sources of data, as secretly as possible. The difficulty in coming up with an exhaustive taxonomy of alt-data is that we know what it is not, but not what it is. For example, IoT

69 (Teoh, et al. 2019)

70 (Quandl Inc. 2020)

sensors are used extensively in manufacturing and logistics. But it is impossible to fully understand what role they will have in the future, for individuals, but also businesses, for instance in monitoring supply chains.

One trend that is obvious and fuelling this explosion of alt-data is the digitisation of individuals' behaviours. We leave – voluntarily or not – digital footprints everywhere. Even in the mundane task of downloading an app on our phones, we consent to – mostly unclear – data collection about everything we do with the service. We get tracked through our phone networks, and each time we communicate through technology. Online, our shopping habits, what we browse, our internet searches, our online discussions and social media activity all constitute new entries in giant databases. Whether we like it or not, the implied agreement here is that it improves our life through enhanced quality of service.

To the neophyte, satellite imaging is often mocked as a spurious source of alt-data. Maybe inspired by the famous story of Sam Walton's counting cars at his Walmart stores from the sky in the 1950s, many people have doubts about such techniques. It is actually an impressive space, as technology has become incredibly sophisticated. Some companies specialise in answering business questions and framing them as problems that can be assessed through satellite imaging. Of course, the drop in the cost of launching satellites has now made them available for commercial purposes. But, it is mostly the advances in AI computer vision that have boosted the field. Computers are now able to track complex objects, for instance what an oil barrel looks like in various lighting conditions or when partially hidden. And, there are many things you can say from continually monitoring what is happening on the ground, in fields like agriculture, mining, oil, metal tracking or maritime traffic. For example, advanced systems can analyse vessel routes, activity at ports, or disruptions in supply chains. That makes for insightful business indicators, at an aggregate or detailed level.

Lastly, and especially in finance, a lot of the alt-data we refer to comes in the form of textual data. Their unstructured data make them particularly rich to analyse. From within an institution, emails, reports, commentaries, and presentations all form a valuable source of data, the challenge being to make sense of it all.

USE CASES FOR ALTERNATIVE DATA

An implicit assumption, so far, is that alt-data may provide an advantage to shrewd traders. Indeed, it is mostly thought of in the context of *alpha generation*. We can assume that most market participants now consume all mainstream data sources, and an edge needs to be found elsewhere. Maybe this is the closest we got to the *Efficient Market Hypothesis* – which assumes that all information is instantaneously incorporated into asset prices. There is still hope for traders to beat the market by exploiting non-readily-available, hard-to-access, or obscure sources of information.

One direct implication for buyers is the need to keep these data sources private, or at least, not to publicise them. This aspect is at odds with the concept of data platforms making datasets available to whoever is willing to pay for them. The risk is that alpha might decay rapidly, as informed traders quickly arbitrage out the source of value.

Maintaining an information advantage through advance indicators of future market movements is a natural use case for alt-data. But, there are, at least, two others. One usage is *nowcasting*. Nowcasting – which was coined in meteorology to characterise very short-term predictions – is the forecasting of current economic conditions, hence the strange-sounding term. Indeed, all macroeconomic variables – and many other economic variables – are released with a significant lag for obvious operational reasons. Here, satellite images, for instance, have been proven to provide very accurate readings of manufacturing PMIs, but with a crucial difference: they are available in real-time.[71] It is an interesting development in terms of response to official data releases. Also, one day, it might be that these so-called alt-data sources will be considered as the more efficient way to provide these economic indicators and leave the remit of alternative data. As evidence of this effect, a recent study[72] showed that the market reaction to earnings surprises was reduced for retailers for which satellite-based estimates of parking lot traffic were available.

Another use case for alt-data is in answering more complex questions, and on much longer horizons than traditional alpha capture. For example, in asset allocation, playing particular investment themes has become popular. But, how would you go about constituting a dynamic portfolio of securities playing, say, the topic of this book, "AI in financial services"? It is easy to define the broad investment universe; in this case, companies operating in the financial sector. But, how would you determine the exposure of a particular company to the theme of AI, and how would you weight it in the portfolio? Also, how would you define rules that can be run automatically depending on the degree of exposure to the theme? There are no divisions within these firms that specifically target AI, and the technology is present in multiple business areas. One way to answer this problem is through alternative datasets, like company press releases, news, possibly academic papers, and patent filings. These are mainly textual data, but by building a vocabulary[73] for the theme and through natural language processing, one can start measuring the exposure of a particular company to the thesis and seize

71 I ignore issues like the handling of cloudy days, for instance
72 (Zhu 2019)
73 It is possible to automatically learn the domain-specific vocabulary from reference texts

the investment accordingly. It is not a perfect answer, but the allocation process can be coded up and is adaptive.

CHARACTERISTICS OF ALTERNATIVE DATA

A good approach when dealing with a new dataset is to pause and think about the value that one can reasonably expect to extract from it. If a subject matter expert cannot articulate a logical thought process that could explain the presumed benefit, a general rule is to steer away from it. In the case of alternative data, there is a higher hurdle to clear. It is not only about identifying the usefulness of the data, but also whether the signal is not already contained in some other readily available datasets. It is unlikely that we can derive much information for short-term trading from an in-depth analysis of a lengthy earnings press release when actual earnings have already hit the screen. However, it could be that, for a longer-term investment, only elements present in the company narrative will have a lasting effect on its performance.

Alternative data can be characterised by the same standard attributes of quality and representativity. It needs to be accurate enough, timely, and cover enough of the market of interest to be useful and not be too biased. But, two features apply specifically to alternative data as opposed to mainstream data. Firstly, its rarity. How easy is it to obtain that data, and in particular, for competitors? In most cases – and indeed, for alpha generation – its dissemination quickly reduces its worth. And secondly, its usability. As alternative data can be found almost anywhere, it is essential to think about how its signal can be exploited. It is not only because information can be extracted from noise, that it is of use. There are many cases where the signal – even though valuable – also contains other factors that cannot be hedged out, rendering the signal of interest impossible to capture.

SPECIFIC RISKS AROUND ALTERNATIVE DATA

Given their disparate nature, alternative datasets, even for the user, present several issues. There is not a body of regulatory work specifically targeting alternative data yet, and extra care should, therefore, be taken. It is not as simple as following prescribed rules, but more a question of a thorough assessment, documentation, and often common sense. As in similar cases, a robust governance framework, including a record of best practices, would go a long way in protecting the organisation that wishes to interact with alternative data.

In financial markets, there are many regulations with the objective to guarantee a fair and well-functioning market. It is always useful to make sure that the specific data complies with the spirit of the regulation. *Data privacy* is also on everyone's mind these days. Particularly when the data collected relates to individuals, it might not be sufficient for the *data collector* just to gather consent. For instance, under GDPR in Europe, there is great concern around the ability to identify an individual – so-called *personal data*. Simple anonymisation techniques might not be sufficient, as multiple data sources might be used to reveal with reasonable accuracy the identity of a person.

I talked previously about gathering data from the internet. This is a practical and powerful way to build valuable alternative datasets. However, the law in most countries about *web scraping* is unclear. Aggressive tactics – like making frequent data requests, or bypassing paywalls – are obviously out of the question. But, beyond this, it is necessary to check whether the data has been acquired in compliance with the T&Cs of the targeted websites. Bots are usually a concern for web servers, so it should be relatively easy to have a first idea of what is authorised or not.[74]

---

74 For instance, adding a /robots.txt at the root of the website is a common practice
(e.g. https://www.example.com/robots.txt)

More complex are issues around *privacy leakage*. What I mean by this is situations where one could expect that particular piece of data to be private. For instance, in our case of the flight routes taken by senior executives at a company, shareholders could easily argue that such information should be kept private. I imagine that exploiting that data for trading purposes – possibly to the detriment of the company – could be legally challenged.[75]

Even more problematic is data that could be seen as *material non-public information* (MNPI). Definitions of what constitutes MNPI differ from jurisdiction to jurisdiction, but it is easy to imagine situations where one is very close to crossing the line. Interestingly, the fact that data could only be collected by very few players with unlimited means to access and analyse the data usually does not make it non-public data. Asymmetries of information are widespread in the investment world. Actually, it is commonly used as an argument by proponents of alternative data. For them, retail investors should not play individual stocks, as they do not have access to the required data to make informed decisions.

Finally, ethical considerations are what should also drive the use of alternative data. If it does not feel right, or if it could be seen in a different light as abusive, discriminatory, improper, unprofessional, etc., it is best to look for signals somewhere else.

---

75 Note that I am just making that case for illustration purposes

9

BUILDING A DATA-DRIVEN ORGANISATION

"Nobody ever saw a dog make a fair and deliberate
exchange of one bone for another with another dog."
                                        Adam Smith

In order to scale data projects, and not leave them as isolated
events, it is fundamental to build a fully data-driven organisation. Management consultants would probably write this piece in
a heart-beat. And, it would certainly be much better than what I
could do. Rightly so, these advisors may say that the change should
not just be a goal pursued by the technology division. It should be
firm-wide and be aligned with the corporate strategy as a whole
to have the best chance of succeeding. Also, it is essential to invest
in people, at all stages, so that they can support the technological
transformation. The focus must be on bringing people together
and fostering collaboration so that people across the company can
work towards a common objective. They may also add that getting the data architecture right from the start is critical to support
the initiative.

All this is correct. But, it is also widely reported, so I will focus
here on the more practical and pedestrian aspects. I will give my

views as a practitioner. We can probably all agree with the broad direction, but where are the traps? Where do things generally go wrong?

ROADMAP TO BURYING DATA-DRIVEN INITIATIVES

I will start by providing you with a surefire way to fail. I doubt you have that particular objective, but you may have, or will, come across parts of this story. It usually begins with a senior executive, as a response to competitive pressure, pushing for being more data-driven as an organisation. However, at various levels of the organisation, many are sceptical about the power of data and analytics. Their story is universally similar. In their group, one day, there was an attempt to get a first data project out. The technology team, or the data science team, got tasked with solving the particular problem. After an incredible amount of struggle, cost and time, the technology team got a product out. There was much excitement amongst users. But, the solution did not do better than the existing tool. It did not improve business performance, and it is no longer used. Everyone is back to the old system, which still does a fair job. So, they will probably argue that, when it comes to this new initiative asked for by senior management, their group will not be the one footing the bill this time. It just did not work.

Let us unpack what this story tells us. The underlying assumption is that data initiatives are hard in finance. Problems are complex to solve, data is scarce, the signal-to-noise ratio is too low, etc. But, in the vast majority of cases, the problem lies somewhere else. The projects fail because the problem was misspecified from the start. Business and technology did not agree with the questions to ask. Truly understanding what the business is after with a data initiative is critical, and nearly always overlooked. A great deal of detail is required to make sure that the team is solving the right problem. Allowing the technology team to answer a vague question on its own, like improving a group's performance, is a recipe for disaster. Even worse, I have seen cases where the technology team is pushing a solution adapted from some other business areas, pretending it is the cure for a problem they do not really understand.

The reason why this happens so frequently is that it is easier to misspecify a problem – in fact, it is easier than failing at solving it. What the technology is aiming for and what the business truly wants are usually two different things. There is not enough time spent at the beginning to ask the common sense questions and make sure that the problem is well understood by all. I will go back to my example of a recommender system for securities. Quite often, the machine learning-based model would find it difficult to beat a naive approach which just recommends the clients who were historically most active in the security. This is understandable, as the larger funds tend to buy a disproportionate amount of the same securities, for reasons of benchmarking, mandate, etc. If the business is after these simple predictions, then there is no need to build a fancy model.

On the contrary, it could be that the actual value is in finding the less active clients that value the recommendations and would also pay more for them. Or, it could be that bringing valuable content to these clients will be rewarded with more trades. In these cases, the advanced recommender is likely to add value. So, the first step should always be about spelling out precisely what the desk wants as an optimal outcome. The technology team cannot infer this on its own as this requires domain expertise.

Also, innovation is hard, especially at the start, so creating a fertile environment for it is essential. Hoping that the technologists can build solutions with minimal involvement from the business is naive. The two teams should be engaged to reach a common goal, as opposed to pointing fingers at times of failure. An adequate organisational structure is helpful for this but building the right culture is even more potent.

CULTURAL CHANGE

The adage "culture eats strategy for breakfast"[76] is overused, but it is also very true. A cultural transformation is necessary for organisations serious about building a data-driven mindset. The meaning of *culture* is best elaborated through its key attributes – *shared, pervasive, enduring, implicit.*[77]

The best way to share a *culture* is to have it embraced by the leadership team. It needs to be voiced by the top management. However, this is not sufficient – the rest of the organisation must also be convinced. At an early stage of AI adoption, it is best to start with highly visible projects – preferably easier to implement – that win adoption across the firm. It is a good idea to have cross-divisional teams, involving every support function in the company, not just businesses, to make sure that everyone understands the common goal and raises concerns. In terms of concrete implementation, a quick delivery schedule, with short development cycles, should be preferred. In startup parlance, the aspiring company should be *agile* before embarking on more ambitious projects. A constant iteration with users is necessary to increase adoption later on, and to reduce apprehension about the technology. *Shared*, also because the business and the technology team should jointly own projects.

A *pervasive* culture starts with people and structure. On the people side, it requires a blend of domain knowledge and technical exper-

---

76 The quote attribution to management consultant Peter Drucker is disputed

77 (Groysberg, et al. 2018)

tise. It is even better if there are team leaders who have both, possibly business people with a firm grasp of technology. On the organisational side, having a *Chief Data Officer* (CDO), or even better a *Chief Data & Analytics Officer* (CDAO) – who ultimately owns these initiatives – is the direction of travel. Accountability to the CEO and the board cements the strategic nature of the transformation. Needless to say, such a data and analytics strategy has to be aligned with the business strategy, to make sure that the projects are meaningful to the company. It is not as simple as selecting the low-hanging fruits. They need to be simple enough at the start of the journey, but also impactful enough for the company performance. Early successes in what truly matters to the firm will create the much-needed ambassadors to push the organisation forward.

A culture is *enduring*, in the sense that it can resist the natural ups and downs of business life. Failure should be acceptable. In itself, failure is informative, as having only successful initiatives probably means that the organisation is not aiming high enough. But more importantly, it helps to create a *culture of innovation*, where failure is not a stigma. Another way to promote innovation is by building a portfolio of AI investments, as opposed to a single initiative. Some will be more successful than others, but this way, there will be a continuous pipeline of projects. Production-ready solutions will replace POCs[78], and POCs will replace mere ideas. Of course, assessing the ROI and impact at the start will still be the gauge for prioritising proposals. Also, promoting innovation does not mean that everything needs to be built in-house. Thinking about a *buy-versus-build* approach is always sound. Generally speaking, buying – at an acceptable cost – is preferable for non-core services, while building is usually cheaper in the long run for core activities.

78 Proofs-Of-Concept

Lastly, an AI culture is *implicit*. What it is all about are mostly unwritten rules. But slowly, data-driven decisions will trump those based on anecdotal evidence. In turn, fact-based choices will be sought by the workforce. And finally, such a culture will attract like-minded people, reinforcing itself in the process.

DATA GOVERNANCE AND DATA ARCHITECTURE

At a more pragmatic level, maximising success requires sound *data governance* and *data architecture*. These involve looking at all aspects of data throughout its lifecycle. Fortunately, data assets needed for AI are not that different from other data assets. Data governance has had a well-established framework for some time now. The only real change is the promotion of the CDO – or CDAO – due to the increased importance of data and analytics within organisations. Strong governance involves the definition of roles and responsibilities for the *data governance committee* (overseen by the CDO) and for the *data stewards* – who own specific datasets and are responsible for data quality, security and usage.

Most issues relevant to the governance framework revolve around a few key topics. There are the data management initiatives themselves, in particular, to improve *data quality*, in terms of accuracy, but also consistency across systems. They require appropriate *data standards*, for instance, ensuring that the same *metadata is* used across the organisation. Then, there is the vital subject of *data access*, as ultimately, data is consumed by users across the firm. And, sometimes it is about managing the various stakeholders, who might have conflicting views about how to handle their data assets.

Once again, the field is now reasonably mature; I will not delve into it. I will instead share what I think are among the best practices. An essential goal of managing data assets is to create a single source of *ground truth* for the organisation. Within financial institutions, it is common to have multiple information systems with possibly conflicting information. This could be due to bad *data lineage*. Tracking and documenting the data flow, including transformations, is critical to not jeopardising the data analysis. It is usually a good idea to store data within *data lakes* so that raw data can be queried later if needed. And, basic *data validation* at entry is also a useful way to avoid problems down the chain. In order to gather useful feedback about access and usage over time, it is helpful to have a monitoring tool and metrics. This helps to improve processes and measure engagement from users and could form a KPI for the people in charge.

I think access rights are also an important part of the culture. When establishing a new information system, I prefer a model that gives access by default to everyone. Portions of the data can be restricted, for instance, when dealing with information on a need-to-know basis – which is common in finance. It is much more powerful this way than the other way round. Naturally, users are inclined to query the system if they have access to it.

Along the same line of thought, I think a two-layer access tool is ideal. First, an attractive GUI,[79] like a standard business intelligence tool, is necessary so that users can easily query the data. But, introducing some sort of scripting language can help build a community of more advanced users, interested in doing their own analysis. They are likely to become the next data ambassadors. Their curiosity will lead to innovation, which in turn will increase the likelihood of answering valuable business questions.

79 A Graphical User Interface is a visual interface with the data system, which is easy to manipulate

ROADMAP TO PROJECT SUCCESS

I talked about the best way to sink a data project. But, what are the key steps to maximising the probability of success? Earlier, I covered some of the necessary steps in a typical pipeline – preparing the data, running multiple candidate models and assessing performance in a robust framework. I will now look at the most overlooked steps that are often correlated with success.

As I mentioned earlier, the vast majority of initiatives fail because of the disconnect between the business and the modelling team. It could be due to multiple reasons, organisational ones, or just bad project management. Regardless of the reason, this initial collaboration phase is the most important of any project. It involves carefully defining the problem in business terms. The first question is about users. Beyond knowing who they are, it is about understanding how they will use the solution. Is it 100% clear how the proposed tool will be integrated into their workflow? It requires us to spell out precisely what the true objective is. Not just at a high level, but to answer the question – what questions do users expect the tool to answer? In which circumstances will it be useful?

A related matter is whether there are already existing solutions to the problem – partly or wholly. A typical example is the existence of an expert system that may have performance issues or may be difficult to maintain. In any case, that will be a useful benchmark to beat. Improving on the existing solutions requires a definition of the performance measure. The metrics – which are often multiple – need to be well crafted to answer the exact questions asked by the business. For instance, in our recommender system, does the business only care about the outright accuracy of predictions? Or, is it also about the diversity of recommendations? Or, is it relevant to look at the overall trades with these clients, irrespective of the precise recommendations? Once we have clear performance measures, it is useful to define a threshold that needs to be reached to validate the solution. It may not be very precise at this stage, but it will help the developers to evaluate their progress.

This first step is also the phase where inputs from *subject matter experts* are the most needed. Inputs related to both the data and the solution are usually required. How would they solve the problem themselves? And, to the best of their knowledge, what data would be necessary to answer the questions? The business can then make an assessment about the availability of the data (at project inception and when the system is live) and its potential cost (upfront and in maintenance terms). Lastly, this is a good time to assess other production-related questions. What is the expected maintenance cost? Is it a system that will require many upgrades? How responsive does it need to be? If used for trading, for instance, it might require a particular architecture – and computational resources – to produce the outputs in time.

Once the required data has been gathered or possibly sampled, the important phase of *data exploration* begins. This is mostly neglected by engineers, as there is the presumption that the model will take care of it. Sometimes it is also because they are not familiar with the data. The solution is not to skip this part, but instead to get inputs from the business. Data exploration should be extensive to have an in-depth understanding of the data complexity. Visualisation may be a powerful way to help with this task. For every single feature, one needs to gather its characteristics, its nature, the percentage of missing values, its distribution, the variance across samples, etc. If in supervised learning, one can also attempt to assess their predictive power – with respect to the output – through correlation analysis or by segmenting the data. Scatter plots of the combinations of two variables are usually informative, too. Measuring distances between data points, to assess representativity, may be telling for some tasks. The precise steps are data- and problem-dependent, but they should not be rushed. Importantly, documenting the results can help engage with the business to assess if the first analysis already reveals something, or if complementary data is needed.

The last phase is about productionising the software – which should have already been prepared at the start – and this requires particular attention. Firstly, one should ensure that the outputs can be consumed easily by the users. The quality of the publishing should be refined enough. Visualisation tools can help, in particular, to further probe the results. It is also good practice to think about the system life cycle at this point. Measurement of software performance over time needs to be scheduled to react to possible drops in quality. How often does the model need to be retrained? Is it necessary to immediately incorporate new information as it becomes available, or is it more a case of making changes in response to a deterioration in performance? This is also the appropriate moment to talk about future model upgrades and the governance around them.

If these three phases of problem definition, data exploration and end-to-end production cycle were less neglected, success rates would undoubtedly be higher. Also, as the teams refine these stages, they become better at implementing them for the next project.

10

AI RISKS

"I believe that whatever we do or live for has its causality; it is good, however, that we cannot see through to it."

Albert Einstein

The *paperclip maximiser* is an advanced AI system. It started its life as an algorithm in a factory producing paperclips. Over time, it became increasingly sophisticated through learning, achieving better results at each generation. It did so by maximising its simple objective function which involved growing its paperclip production. All resources on earth, including human beings – and later the whole universe – are used by the superintelligent paperclip maximiser. Earth is now populated by paperclips only. Exterminating humans was a perfectly rational outcome of the maximiser's optimisation function – as humans might have been tempted to switch off the machines.

This is a story told by AI thought-leader Nick Bostrom.[80] The anecdote illustrates some of the risks in AI. One is the risk that machine intelligence might not be aligned with our human goals, in particular, preserving human life. The other is that there could be a point where AI systems are so advanced in their cognitive abilities that humans would no longer be able to tame their expansion.

---

80 (Bostrom, Ethical issues in advanced artificial intelligence. 2003)

These are important ethical considerations that many AI experts think should be addressed alongside the development of the technology. Even in the short term, there are risks to AI systems which are critical to understand, also because some of these risks are on the radar of regulators around the world. I have already covered some of the data issues so I will focus on AI-only dangers.

It is worth noting that AI regulation is mostly non-existent. Most countries have so far tried to adapt existing legislation to capture these emerging risks. But, some risks are undoubtedly specific to the inner mechanisms and the complexity of the field and require particular attention. Economic considerations also complicate the discourse. Every government – starting with the US and China – is convinced of the incredible potential of AI technologies in terms of future growth, and would not want to miss out by regulating it too stringently.

EXPLAINABILITY

What good is a technology that you do not understand? One specificity of AI is its inner workings. Somewhat strangely, reading the source code of an AI system would not tell you what the machine does. You would comprehend the learning mechanism and what the program is solving for, but you would not know what it has learnt. This is problematic in many use cases. It is even outright illegal in some regulated activities, where explanations or human oversight are required. For instance, under GDPR in Europe, "the data subject shall have the right not to be subject to a decision based solely on automated processing".[81]

Neglecting these issues might, therefore, expose the firm to legal challenges. It could also present a risk of economic loss. For instance,

81 (The European Parliament and the Council 2016)

it could be that computers make wrong decisions that their opera-tors cannot correct because they do not understand how they were formed in the first place. Generally speaking, poor comprehension will result in a lack of trust in the models, possibly neglecting their benefit. It is why explainable AI (XAI) has become such an import-ant topic. Models can no longer be pure black-boxes, or they will not reach their full potential.

Explainable AI may be seen as an ethical consideration, but it is also a practical one. Understanding the *why* may be the differ-ence between models that work and opaque models that fail. It is about designing systems that reach the desired outcome. This usually means fairer models, with fewer biases, and ultimately less risk in a broad sense.

Explainable AI is an abundant field of research, and we are only seeing the beginning. Ideally, explaining the *why* revolves around *causality*. A typical trait of human intelligence is our ability to form *cause-effect* connections. We actually do this with reasonable ease (in simple settings). This ability to reason is incredibly hard for machines. In particular, it cannot be reduced to basic correlations. As we know too well, it is not because two phenomena happen in a synchronised manner that a cause-effect relationship exists. There is plenty of evidence around us of spurious correlations. Mathe-matically, it is easy to build correlated series, even driven by statis-tically independent variables.[82] Also, trending prices in finance, for instance, might lead to high correlation. Here, it is more the pres-ence of common causes that may lead to the two variables trending simultaneously. Quantitative easing by central banks has made us familiar with such examples. Nonetheless, in the vast majority of

---

82 Forming ratios from three independent variables is a popular example of spurious correlations

cases, there is no reason to imply any causation. There might be a common cause – named a *confounder* – to the two series but no cause-effect relationship between them.

So, what is so tricky about inferring *causation*? At this point, it is useful to borrow the framework of Judea Pearl, a Turing Award[83] recipient who has made significant contributions to the field of causality. One way to look at correlation versus causation is to think in terms of *seeing* versus *doing*. Seeing two phenomena happening together in a correlated fashion is just an observation. Causality requires us to conduct a first action that itself produces the second phenomenon. Pearl talks about three levels of causal inference. [84] The most basic level is called *association* and corresponds to *seeing*. In other words, how does my observation of X change my belief in Y? The second level is the *doing* and is purposely named *intervention*. It answers *what-if* questions and requires action X to be performed before observing Y. The highest level in the *causal hierarchy* is the *counterfactuals*. It involves taking alternative actions to truly understand the *why*.

There is a well-known approach in scientific studies to attempt to reach the higher levels of causality – or *explainability* in AI. It is called *randomised controlled trials* (RCT). In medical studies, the procedure randomly allocates patients to two groups, with one usually receiving a placebo and the other getting an intervention. In this manner, one attempts to remove spurious correlations of other factors and focus on the actual effect of the treatment. This works because it requires taking an action – and comparing the result to a control group. This is in opposition to *observational studies*, where the researchers can only access already collected data without the ability to conduct new tests.

83 In simple terms, the Turing Award is the Nobel Prize of Computing
84 (Pearl, The seven tools of causal inference, with reflections on machine learning. 2019)

This is where the issue of AI explainability in finance is the most evident. There is no equivalent to an RCT in finance. Except in rare cases, we cannot run new experiments in finance. We cannot rerun a market crash with different actions. We cannot run a company differently and see what would have happened. We can only observe data that already exists, and try to infer causal relationships from this.

INTERPRETABILITY

There is a large body of work that aims to extract cause-effects from observational data, but most current tools in explainable AI are about *interpretability*. *Interpretability* is apprehending what the system does. Not the *why*, yet, but the first step towards understanding. To do so, it is relatively easy to see what our options are.

Firstly, we could use simple models. Linear models – or more generally interpretable models – would give us interpretability for free. For instance, a decision tree model would be easy to read for a human. However, it would defy the purpose of machine learning, as there would not be much learning in the process. The models would be too simplistic for most concrete problems. I am still mentioning this option, as many regulated activities use such straightforward models for reason of interpretability.

Then, we could look at the role of different variables – or features – in relation to the output. This is always a good idea and involves some sort of *sensitivity analysis* across the range of the input variable to see its impact on the output. The main drawback is that these techniques[85] look at variables independently, which does not capture the full richness in the data. Some models also have some built-in measure of feature importance. For instance, in a decision tree, or collection of trees,

85 The two standard techniques are *Partial Dependence Plot* (PDP) and *Individual Conditional Expectation* (ICE)

one can rank the features in decreasing order of the information that they bring in building the tree.

Constructing *white-box models* – by opposition to *black-box models* – is another route. For instance, once we have trained a complex model, a black-box, we could learn an interpretable model, like a decision tree, that would approximate the sophisticated model as closely as possible. The objective is to learn as refined a model as possible while translating it in a second step into a simpler one. It might not be apparent at first, but this is better than starting with a basic model on the data itself. One limitation is that we learn a model of a model, as opposed to a model of the data, and we may also lose valuable information in the process. This approach is called *global surrogate* modelling.

The other route to white-box modelling is to adapt complex models – with the hope that we can keep their advanced properties – but tweaking them so that they become *more* interpretable. One example is to constrain the relationship between inputs and output in a monotonic fashion.[86] So, the output can only increase – or decrease – with the input variable, instead of being able to take any functional form. In many cases, phenomena might not be linear, but monotonicity might not be unrealistic.

The last option is also the most commonly used in practice.[87] The idea is similar to our global surrogate model, but it only applies the concept *locally*. It means that one approximates by an interpretable model close to a given data point alone. For that given observation, the model becomes highly understandable. This is desirable for the business, as we can now easily explain the model drivers for a given prediction. It is impossible to translate the overall model into a sin-

---

86 In particular, I have in mind the imposition of monotonic constraints in Gradient Boosting

87 The two common techniques are *Local Interpretable Model-agnostic Explanations*, known as *LIME*, and computing *Shapley values*

gle equation, but locally, this becomes possible. *Local interpretability* has the benefit of combining sophisticated modelling – for the phenomenon at play – with explainability of decisions at a local level. For instance, it would be impossible to explain the overall pricing of an insurance policy. But, when a customer questions the price she received, it would be possible to provide an explanation for her specific quote. One reason for the success of these methods is that they are model-agnostic. They can be applied to even the most sophisticated algorithms – for instance neural networks – while still providing the same benefits.

For regulatory purposes, I would like to make a case for local explainability (the last option). Undoubtedly, AI brings value to complex problems in the form of more advanced models that can capture a complicated reality. This cannot be achieved with simple modelling, and it is not beneficial to impose such constraints. If we can add explainability – even if it is only in a restricted area – we achieve significant progress in better serving our customers. They receive a higher quality product – thanks to a more refined model – and they can still question it if necessary. In the absence of major breakthroughs in the field, I believe this is a valuable first step for practical AI even in the most sensitive areas.

COMBATTING BIASES

What are the odds that a computer, when deciding whether to hold or to sell a security, will start discarding all negative news to keep only the positive news? Zero. Machines are not subject to behavioural biases, that we, humans, frequently exhibit, like in the above example, *confirmation bias*. In that sense, they are superhuman. They do not sleep, they do not fail,[88] they do not make mistakes. Fundamentally, they do not have the limitations of our biological bodies and the hormones dictating our emotions. So, without a doubt, they are a better version of us, with the ability to correct our biases.

This is largely true, but not always. In some cases, they might perpetuate existing biases in the data, and even exacerbate them. Regulators are worried about fairness and non-discrimination, especially in activities targeting individuals and especially within certain demographic groups. Lending and insurance decisions, and, to a lesser extent, customer recommendations, are primary areas of regulatory scrutiny. The reality is that – for reasons that we do not fully comprehend – machine learning techniques may be efficient at picking up these subtle biased effects. If there is a particular discrimination at play in a dataset, it could be that the algorithm will find it optimal to compound the prejudice. While a human being, animated by such a bias, might restrain any excessive behaviour, the machine will not be driven by any moral compass.

Such biased conduct is derived from mimicking human actions. But, there are other reasons for biases. For instance, a lack of representativity in the data collection may perpetuate certain traits. One example is in sampling data, where certain populations may be underrepresented or overrepresented, which will ultimately affect predictions. Outdated or incomplete data may prevent the model from achieving an optimal outcome, too. I will later cover the case of *overfitting* or *concept drift* – which are not biases per se – but can still lead to poor results. However, in these particular cases, robust testing will help control these issues.

The debate around machines addressing our human biases, or instead exacerbating them, is ongoing. At any rate, the best cure is robust governance control. It is essential to test for fairness in high-risk situations.

---

88 At least, not as commonly as we do

Explainability of outcomes is also crucial in identifying biases before correcting them. When deploying AI, it is necessary to invest in these topics, as they will increasingly become top of the agenda for regulators, and rightly so. To reap the benefits of AI, it is best to address its possible shortcomings early on.

ALGORITHMS VULNERABILITY

In finance, AI is already extensively used for fraud detection, AML[89] or algorithmic trading. Despite their complexity, these algorithms are still deterministic, and their decision process could technically be reverse-engineered. They are advanced pattern recognition systems, and, with enough resources, they may be subject to attacks. This is nothing new in the world of cybersecurity, and it can apply to AI systems too.

There comes a point where resources are cheap enough, and the technology sophisticated enough, to shift the balance of incentives. Cybercriminals, money launderers and rogue traders might find sufficient reward in attempting to dupe AI systems. For instance, after sufficiently repeated attempts, bots may learn the most discriminatory aspects in a given decision taken by a machine, and they may exploit the flaw in order to deceive the machine. If there are ways to interpret what an algorithm does, as we have seen previously, it is feasible for a badly-intentioned person to learn that representation.

Fortunately, it is still incredibly challenging to do so in practice, for operational reasons in particular, but this is a battle that can never stop. As more decisions are handled by machines over time, addressing vulnerability in machine processing should become a growing area of attention.

89 Anti-Money Laundering

OUTSOURCING DECISIONS TO MACHINES

Handing over the decisions to machines has its own set of issues. Of course, there are still many places – probably the majority – where humans will be involved for a long time to come. In most cases, the human-machine combination is the best practical solution. The computers can do 80% of the work, the heavy-lifting part which requires substantial processing power, and the specialists can handle the remaining 20%, which needs the full breadth of our intelligence.

Nonetheless, there are places where involving humans in the decision process is not practical. Frequent trading and market-making, through automated pricing, are two areas that come to mind. In trading, machines process new information and react accordingly with particular trading decisions. The complication here is that their response time to new data is incredibly fast. Also, as multiple machines treat the same – or mostly similar – data, there is a high probability that they will learn the same patterns. In some situations, it might create an overreaction from the machines, which may attempt, for instance, to place the same orders at the same time. The uniformity of machine architectures and algorithms, coupled with the same trading data feeding them, may create a systemic risk when the balance of market participants is geared towards automated trading systems. The solution is naturally human oversight to prevent machines from overreacting. However, this is a much harder task than it seems. Given their intricate mechanisms, such intervention may be beyond human reach. Stepping in or not, when to do it, and what to do are all valid questions that are not easily solved. It is definitely more complicated than adding circuit-breakers that switch off the machines. It is unclear whether we, humans, will be better at managing these crises than the machines.

In market-making, it makes sense to let algorithms handle the more mundane tasks, like pricing smaller ticket sizes. This is a perfect area, where data – structured or not – can be processed and analysed much more accurately by machines. It is not difficult to imagine a world where algorithms increasingly derive pricing. It is already the case in many corners of retail, like the more straightforward case of pricing plane tickets. So, algorithmic pricing is already a reality, and soon this will be the case in finance too.

One area of concern, though, is that machines may be better at colluding than humans. For instance, a recent study[90] showed that algorithms might be colluding by charging *supra-competitive* prices without even communicating with one another. This *tacit collusion* is often explained with a simple example. If a machine expects another algorithm to match its price discount, it might lose the incentive to reduce its price in the first place. In other words, machines may reach oligopoly, even in competitive environments. The study, and similar ones, is obviously idealised. The market is simplified. For instance, the time to learn such optimal behaviours is unrealistically long. But, the outcome is still instructive, and undoubtedly, antitrust bodies will watch the development of algorithmic pricing in these regulated markets.

Regulators care most about systemic risks. We have seen that some market crashes may be attributed to algorithmic trading. In risk management, market participants may also rely on machines to assess risk. This could cause regulatory issues if risks end up being misrepresented or misunderstood. I am far from arguing that the technology is not contributing to social good. It has undeniable merits in terms of removing some of the market inefficiencies – that may just arise from the human condition itself. But, it

90 (Calvano, et al. 2019)

is naive, and also dangerous, to think that we can further develop the science without spending a significant amount of resources to understand it, control it, and ultimately make it safer. We have seen the same story repeating itself many times in technological innovation before.

PART THREE
TECHNICAL AI

11

THINKING LIKE A MACHINE LEARNING ENGINEER

"You don't understand anything until you learn it more than one way."

Marvin Minsky

This book aims to provide the reader with an intuition for the many phenomena at play. The goal here is to develop an instinct rather than maintaining scientific rigour. If over time, these modelling concepts become second nature, they will be incredibly valuable for the practitioner who wants to be part of the journey. That deeper understanding will stimulate imagination and creativity. The entire field will become more unified, and parallels between apparently unrelated problems and solutions will be easier to identify.

These more advanced notions do not need to be thoroughly understood immediately, but, by going back to them, they will progressively show their merit and value. My goal, for now, is to introduce them to you in a way that feels like common sense. Hopefully, if presented in the right context, many of these concepts will trigger an "of course" or "makes sense" from you. Internalising these will be a first step towards encoding them into your intuition.

This exercise could carry on and on. As more advanced concepts are being introduced, they will form the basis for more subtle ones. I have therefore made a choice to select only the themes that have a broad application in the field of machine learning, but again, this is largely subjective.

GENERALISATION, REGULARISATION AND MODEL SPARSITY

It is now clear that one of the secret weapons of machine learning is the framework around creating models that generalise well. Testing models on unseen data is the assurance that we are not overfitting the training data, that we are not extracting noise from the learning samples.

But what if we do? Usually, machine learning engineers test their model on a test set, but also on the train set. What we are after is a situation where the performance on the train and test sets is similar. If this is the case, it means that what the model learned on the training data will perform well on new data. It is also possible that the performance on the test set will be much worse than on the train set.[91] This would mean that the learning has not been good enough.

One potential explanation is that the model is too complex. It is trying too hard to fit the training data and, in doing so, captures unrepresentative patterns in the data – or, noise. You have encountered this, when on a chart, the modeller plots a line that attempts to go through too many points, rather than choosing a simpler line, and all this does is overfit to noisy data.

---

91 Note that the reverse would be peculiar, as it would mean that the model does better on unseen data!

Overfitting

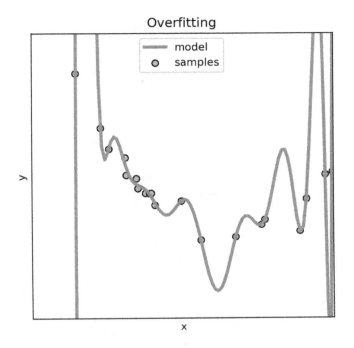

About right

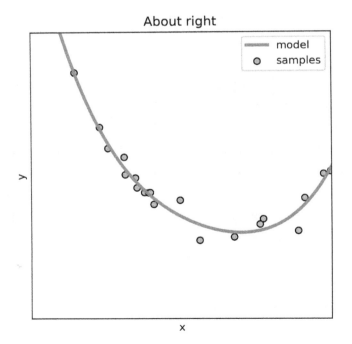

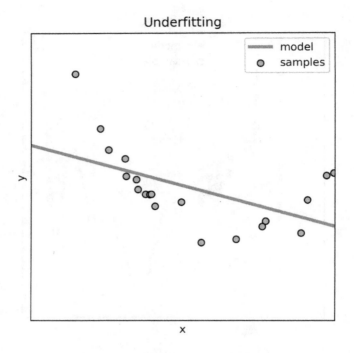

Figure 3 – model complexity illustration of overfitting/underfitting

One way to make a model simpler is to have fewer parameters or less dominant parameters: this is called *regularisation*. Let me explain how this works. If in a simple regression, a given parameter, as estimated by the training exercise, has a very large value, it means that a small change in the input will yield a substantial change in the output. That is not a desirable outcome when it comes to generalisation. Somehow, two samples with little difference in one input variable will lead, according to our model, to vastly different predictions. So, the solution is to constrain the parameters so that they cannot take large values. To achieve this – and this is a prevalent technique in optimisation – we just add a *regularisation term* in our objective function, which penalises large values of the parameters. As the optimisation algorithm attempts to minimise our objective function, it will do so by favouring smaller value parameters.

Of course, reducing the weight of a parameter could go all the way to 0, which means removing that variable altogether. Promoting models with fewer variables (or features) is called encouraging *model sparsity*, and is very common in data modelling. We prefer simpler models, because they probably capture more of the essence in the data, and generalise better.

As an alternative, we could also have manually tried multiple models with fewer parameters. But, as we have just seen, we can do better by using a framework to force a model to be simpler. Two models do just that. *Ridge Regression*[92] promotes parameters of similar magnitude, while *LASSO Regression*[93] encourages sparsity (fewer parameters).

Note that another source of poor generalisation could be that, over time, the target variable has statistical properties that change. For example, the structure of the market has evolved, and the relationships at play to predict a given market variable are no longer good enough. This effect is called *concept drift* and requires a retraining of the model or similar actions to capture the new dynamic.

BIAS-VARIANCE TRADE-OFF

If we have a simpler model, we saw that it might generalise better. In other words, the model exhibits low *variance*. This means that the model does not have much sensitivity to small changes in the training data, and therefore has not captured irrelevant aspects in the data. However, having too simple a model could lead to high *bias*. That indicates that the quality of the predictions might not be

---

92 Ridge and LASSO regressions use respectively a l2-norm and a l1-norm in the penalty term

93 LASSO: Least Absolute Shrinkage and Selection Operator

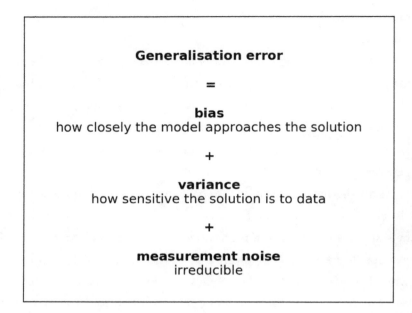

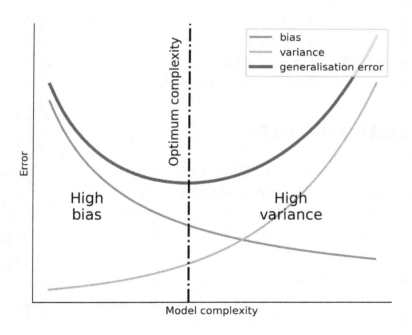

Figure 4 – decomposition of the generalisation error

great as the model might be too simple to capture the richness in the data.

In general, there is a trade-off between bias and variance. The lower the variance (think a simpler model), the higher the bias, and vice versa. It can be shown that the generalisation error rate is a combination of three elements: bias (how closely the model approaches the solution), variance (how sensitive the solution is to data), and measurement noise (which is related to capturing imperfect data). While we cannot reduce measurement noise using the same data, the choice of model is often driven by the motivation to reduce bias or variance, without affecting the other too much.

The bias-variance trade-off is a crucial consideration in model validation. It is commonly referred to as dealing with *underfitting* (high bias) versus *overfitting* (high variance).

BACK TO OBJECTIVE FUNCTIONS

What we called the objective function – when trying to simplify the model through regularisation – was the sum of a *goodness-of-fit* term, which deals with the quality of the prediction, and a *penalty term*, which was there to control the complexity/overfitting of the model. In minimising the objective function, we attempt to reduce both this prediction error term (goodness-of-fit) and the overfitting (penalty on parameter weights), the balance between the two being controlled by an additional user-defined hyperparameter.

It is quite common in optimisation problems in machine learning to have these two terms, one to naively improve learning, and one to achieve some other objective (like parameter regularisation in the above cases). We note that, given the slightly different concepts at play here, machine learning practitioners interchangeably use the terms: *loss*, *cost* or *objective* functions. Despite not being exact synonyms, you may use either term when asking the engineer about the concrete measure of learning performance.

CROSS-VALIDATION

An alternative and intuitive way of handling overfitting (or lowering bias) is to repeat training multiple times on different parts of the dataset, in a process called *cross-validation*. The common implementation is the *k-fold cross-validation* which involves partitioning the original dataset in k equal-sized samples. Each sample is then used as a test set, while the remaining *k-1* examples constitute the train set. That process is repeated k times, and the generalisation (testing) error is averaged out over the k calculations. That procedure is very efficient at lowering the risk of getting a good result *by chance* on a particular test set, as each sample in the dataset is used at some point as part of the test set.

Of course, the repeated training runs come at the expense of higher computational time (k times higher). Also, variations of cross-validation exist to deal with sequential data (where the test set should always be after the train set), as well as when one wants to preserve particular data properties between train and test sets (like keeping a similar ratio between the classes in a classification task).

FEATURE ENGINEERING

In a related topic about generalisation, it is intuitive to think that the richness of the data collected matters in the quality of the predictions. If we have more *features* to describe any data instance, we should be able to build more refined models.

This is both true and false and covers the vast field of *feature engineering*. Yes, of course, if we have too little information, we will not be able to make accurate predictions. If we only have the performance of the stock market the previous day, it will be impossible to infer the likely direction of the market the next day. At the other extreme, though, if we have every security, economic data, and piece of news as inputs to our model, it is likely that the model will overfit the data. The model has so much information that, if given enough freedom, it will recognise patterns that are unrepresentative of the real drivers of market performance. The model will pick up noise. We already know that model sparsity (fewer parameters or variables) leads to reduced overfitting.

But sometimes, it is helpful to guide the machine. The domain expert, especially in finance, should be able to exert her judgment to determine which piece of data to include. This is a crucial step that should not be underestimated, and unfortunately, too often is. There is this misguided belief that the machine should be able to figure out by itself what is of relevance. It is true when data is in abundance, but less so in concrete finance cases. Also, why would you discard the knowledge of human experts?

Beyond this, what are the other means to obtain a well-balanced dataset? One way, which is commonly used when features have no meaning – for instance in anonymised datasets – is to use dimensionality reduction techniques. These methods combine the most relevant features in a logical way, so as to lose as little information as possible. The drawback is that these combinations of features are no longer interpretable by an observer. Another way is to remove *correlated* features (that carry substantially the same information as other features), *low-variance* features (whose values do not vary much across samples and therefore convey little information), or *sparse* features (features with too many missing values). Lastly, there exist brute-force methods, generically called *feature selection*, that try various combinations of features to see what works best in practice.

CURSE OF DIMENSIONALITY

For a given dataset, having too few parameters is not good, but too many is not good either. So, what is the optimal number of features? Or, expressed in another way, let us say that if we have a number of features (number of dimensions) that we want to use, what is the minimum number of data samples that we should collect? These are very concrete questions in day-to-day machine learning problems.

Unfortunately, there is no single answer. For instance, it depends on the complexity of the task at hand, and the representativity of the data samples collected. But, it also touches on a fundamental aspect of machine learning implementation, *the curse of dimensionality*. Unfortunately, this aspect is too often overlooked by practitioners and leads to poorly specified problems and unrealistic expectations. In its general form, the curse of dimensionality refers to phenomena that arise in high-dimensional spaces, and not so in lower dimensions. We refer, here, to (geometric) spaces, as a data sample can be represented as a point in a space, whose number of dimensions corresponds to the number of features. The more features in the data, the higher the dimensions of the space these data points live in.

In these spaces, many things may appear weird or, at least, unintuitive. For instance, if we were to measure the average distance between data points (samples of the dataset), it increases dramatically with the number of dimensions. Beyond a small number of dimensions, that space looks particularly empty (or very *sparse* in mathematical terms). Indeed, it requires many more data points to equally *fill the space*, when one moves from a segment (1D) to a square (2D), to a cube (3D), etc. So, the ability to distinguish between these points, or find structure, quickly vanishes.

Another way to look at it is by comparing the volume of a ball to its embedding cube while increasing the number of dimensions.

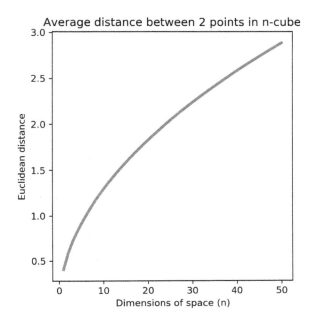

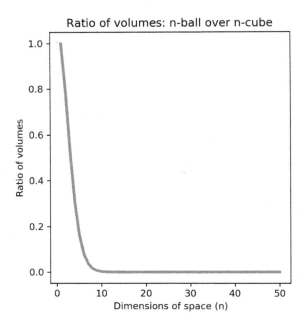

Figure 5 – illustration of the curse of dimensionality

In 3D, the ball fills 52% of its embedding cube (down from 79% in 2D, and 100% in 1D). In 10D, that number is 0.25%! Thus, in high dimension, the probability of encountering a close neighbour – as measured by falling within the unit ball – is negligible. Also, it can be proven[94] that, with increased dimensionality, the distance from a data point to its nearest neighbour approaches the distance to the farthest data point. In these high-dimensional spaces, all points suddenly appear very distant, compromising any attempt to find similarities in the data.

On a concrete level, it implies that, as one increases the number of features to keep, one needs to collect exponentially more data. The exponential nature of this effect makes it a lost cause: it is increasingly difficult to collect enough data, as the number of features increases. This phenomenon must be kept in mind, when deciding on the right dimensionality of a problem, especially in the context of relatively small datasets. Domain expertise, feature engineering, regularisation, and other techniques to control dimensionality all come into their own.

BATCH, MINI-BATCH, STOCHASTIC AND ONLINE LEARNING

Moving away from model generalisation considerations, a concrete concern of machine learning engineers is computational time and resource allocation. This especially applies to large datasets, but also to complex models. For instance, in the popular gradient descent algorithm to solve our objective function minimisation, the algorithm takes many successive steps to converge to a solution. Each time that involves making a series of calculations. In its naive implementation, that means computing that *gradient* (or

---

94 (Weber and Böhm 2000)

derivative) on the entire train set to figure out which direction is the steepest descent. This is called *batch learning*, as it encompasses the full batch of data. If the dataset is significant – and/or the gradient approximation intricate – that becomes costly in terms of computational time and resources.

Stochastic learning is the simplest solution to this. It does the calculation on a single, random (*stochastic*) data point at each step. As the algorithm performs the computation on one sample only, it is only capturing a tiny portion of the dataset information, and therefore the progression, on a walk down the mountain, is very erratic. However, it is fast and works well in practice to approach the solution. This is how one can now handle massive datasets.[95]

For completeness, I will mention *mini-batch learning*, which is in between batch (full dataset) and stochastic (single instance), and which performs the calculations on a small number of random samples (tens or hundreds of data points) at a time. Given the modern hardware architectures of computers, it is still quick,[96] and the convergence[97] is smoother than in the pure stochastic case.

On a related subject, only using small quantities of data (mini-batches) for training may be beneficial elsewhere too. In cases where learning needs to be updated regularly, as new information comes in, incremental learning may be useful. *Online learning* is the process by which learning happens sequentially and gradually. New data points arrive and are used to update the model. A *learning rate* controls the pace of this new learning. This type of learning can be used, for instance, in real-time applications like trading.

---

95 The key consideration here is that, with stochastic learning, computational time no longer grows with the size of the training data

96 Matrix multiplications are very efficient when using GPUs

97 Note that speed of convergence is also controlled by an important hyperparameter, the *learning rate*. This leads to the entire field of *learning rate scheduling*

RANDOMNESS

I will use the topic of stochastic learning to make a point about an almost philosophical question, *randomness*. So far, we have assumed that we are dealing with well-behaved objective functions, in the sense that the procedure of gradient descent would converge towards a single minimum, called a *global minimum*.[98] But, in real life, the algorithm could get stuck in a *local minimum*. Somewhere, there could exist a lower minimum which would provide a better solution to our learning problem. In that context, the erratic nature of stochastic (or mini-batch) learning, due to the randomness of the samples selected at each step, could become an advantage. It may help the algorithm *jump out* of these local minima, and look for a better solution elsewhere. The simple fact of adding randomness in the process might have alleviated a very complex problem in numerical optimisation. In practice – even though this is more relevant in deep learning – that mechanism works.

In other areas too, randomness is a tool used to explore the space of possibilities. For instance, in reinforced learning, where the agent looks for optimal actions to earn an ultimate reward, from time to time and on purpose, the agent makes a random move. Without this, there might be situations where the agent quickly learns a way to the reward, which is not *globally* optimal. The solution could be improved. In forcing the agent to look elsewhere at times, it can explore a broader range of possibilities.

Similarly, in *genetic algorithms*, as new generations are being created, a *mutation rate* is being introduced. Despite inheriting most of their genes from their *parents*, the *children* experience mutations too. Adding a small possibility of genetic modification may lead to overall superior solutions.

---

98 Dealing with convex functions ensures that there is a global minimum

ANOTHER LOOK AT PERFORMANCE METRICS

A performance metric, as the term suggests, is used to assess the overall quality of a model. Sometimes it might be the same as the objective function, and sometimes not. In a business context, you could try to match the ultimate goal of the business unit in terms of performance expectation. For example, when predicting a security price, the mean squared error[99] – and also the mean absolute error[100] – commonly used in regression tasks, could be exactly what the desk wants as a measure of success. These metrics compute the difference between predicted and traded price, on average and in terms of standard deviation.

One area where an objective function for learning may differ from that for overall performance metrics is in classification tasks. The standard performance measure is *accuracy* which is simply the proportion of test samples classified correctly. It is simple enough. However, let us consider a situation where the goal is to predict loans that will lead to default – a form of credit scoring, with two classes: default and non-default. The proportion of defaulted loans in the dataset is, for instance, 5%. Without even using a model, we could predict that all loans will be performing and obtain a 95% accuracy. That is obviously of little use. The problem is that the dataset is significantly *imbalanced*: one class is much more prevalent than the other.

Also, in this specific task, we are really after avoiding defaulted loans as much as possible. So, a more relevant measure could be the proportion of defaulted loans correctly identified, also called *true positive rate,*[101] *recall* or *sensitivity*. In our dummy model, classifying all

99 Usually abbreviated as MSE

100 Usually abbreviated as MAE

101 TPR = TP / (TP + FN), where TP = true positives, FN = false negatives, "positives" being the class of interest

loans as *performing*, the recall would be 0%, which is obviously unacceptable. Now, if we wanted to maximise recall, we could classify all loans as *defaulted* and get a recall of 100%. But, this time again, it would be useless as a model. So, when simple accuracy is not good enough as a measure, one needs to find a balance between *recall* and *precision*.[102] Precision captures how selective our identification of the class of interest is. An all-encompassing performance measure could then be the *Precision-Recall curve* (or similarly the *Receiving Operating Characteristic*, ROC, curve). These are obtained by varying a threshold to reflect the importance of *precision* versus *recall*.

HYPERPARAMETER TUNING

Hyperparameter tuning is an essential part of improving model performance. Hyperparameters are input by the users and control things like model complexity, its architecture, or the optimisation parameters. Sometimes, increasing a given hyperparameter helps with generalisation (possibly at the expense of computational time), or, in other situations, reducing it is more appropriate. It may also be important to find the optimal value. For instance, the learning rate in gradient descent – which deals with the size of the steps at each iteration – cannot be too low or too high. Set too low, and the optimisation algorithm will take too long to converge. Set too high, and it may miss the minimum.

To approach hyperparameter tuning, one can either manually set the parameters or let an algorithm do the optimisation. Setting hyperparameters manually, or at least trying a couple of values, requires the user to understand how they impact model performance. In more straightforward cases, this may be an option. For more compli-

---

102 Precision = TP / (TP + FP), where TP = true positives, FP = false positives

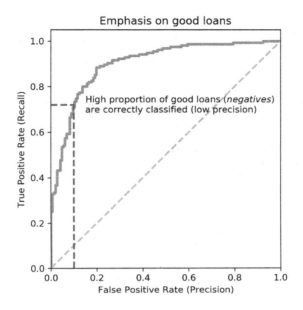

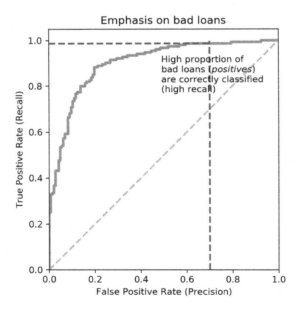

Figure 6 – ROC curves for a credit scoring classification task. Two different thresholds are shown to be more or less selective on one or the other class. Note that positives refer to the default class, which is standard practice.

cated cases, using an automatic way to choose the hyperparameters is needed. The brute-force technique implies a *grid search*, which tries all possible combinations of hyperparameters within specific ranges of user-defined values. The problem is the explosion of the number of combinations. For instance, with 5 hyperparameters and 4 possible values, we are talking about running model training 1,024 times! In many cases, that is impossible, or inefficient, to do. The alternative is to use a *random search*, which employs more or less advanced techniques to guide the search.

BAYES' THEOREM AND BELIEF UPDATES

From the beginning, I took the decision to limit as much as possible the time spent covering mathematical concepts behind machine learning, and instead to focus on intuition. But Bayes' theorem is so ubiquitous in the field that it deserves to be reviewed on its own. Away from machine learning, it is useful to know the rule to understand a prevalent human bias, the *base rate fallacy*, as studied and popularised by psychologists Daniel Kahneman and Amos Tversky.[103]

Looking at a particular application of Bayes' theorem[104] may help. Let us assume your analyst, at a macro fund, comes to you in a state of agitation, stating that you need to buy oil calls immediately. His argument is that he has extensively reviewed news briefs on days of oil crises and something quite remarkable almost always happens. On these days, where oil future prices shoot up by more than 10% within a day, there is – in 99%[105] of the cases – a mention

---

103 (Kahneman and Tversky 1973)

104 Bayes' theorem: $P(H|E) = P(E|H) \times P(H) / P(E)$, where H is the hypothesis and E the evidence

105 The numerical values in this example are purely fictitious, and for illustration purposes only

of the words "war", "tensions in the Middle East", and some other related terms. The analyst adds that some of these words are all over the news today, and therefore one should hedge with oil calls, as the market reaction must be imminent. After looking yourself at that simple piece of data for a few minutes – key words on days of market tension and on normal days – you calmly reply that the fund would be out of business very quickly if you were to follow his advice and buy a hedge. Given the evidence, you conclude that the probability of such market reaction today is a mere 9% – far from a sure win.

What you have done is to simply apply Bayes' theorem to the data available. The first mistake made by the analyst is to confuse two probabilities – the probability of the *hypothesis given the facts*, and the probability of the *facts given the hypothesis*. What we are looking for here is the probability of an oil crisis given certain words in the news – which is low (calculated as being 9%). It is not the same as the probability of these words, given that an oil crisis has been observed – which is very high, at 99%. They have a very different meaning, but our intuition commonly mixes them up.

Our starting assumption – called a *prior probability* – should be the probability of an oil crisis in the absolute. An oil crisis is a rare event, for instance happening in 1% of trading days. Bayes' theorem enables us to *update* that probability based on that new *evidence* – in our case, certain words being present in the news. This is why Bayes' theorem is commonly tasked with updating our beliefs. In our example, the probability of such an oil crisis indeed increases considerably with the presence of these specific terms in the news. But from 1% to 9% only!

Once you have got your head around it, it is actually quite obvious (but, still not intuitive). Let us assume we have 1,000 trading days. Such an oil crisis happens in 1% of the cases, so 10 trading days, of which 9.9 are days where the particular words are mentioned in the news. Out of the other 990 trading days, let us assume that these specific words still appear in 10% of the cases – so a lot less than in 99% of the cases. That is 99 *normal days*, during which these words could be mentioned, for instance in a different context. So, the probability of a trading day, with these particular words mentioned in the news, being the day of an oil crisis is just 9%.[106] The fact that such crises are rare (*base rate*), coupled with the fact that these words may still appear in different contexts, is the reason for the unexpected result.

In other situations, Bayes' theorem may be used in *Bayesian inference*, whereby the objective is to update our belief regarding certain model parameters, in the presence of new data. Bayes' theorem tells us that the probability of these parameters, given the latest data, is proportional to the *likelihood* of this data, given the parameters, *times* the initial probability of the parameters. Or, more concisely: "posterior is proportional to likelihood times prior". We see that, in such learning, we are able to update our knowledge of the parameters, from the likelihood that this new data is generated by these parameters.

A MACHINE LEARNING MODEL FROM SCRATCH

Let us go back to our example of an oil crisis for a moment. Based on the same data, the question could now be: "if one observes these particular words in the news, is it more likely to be a day of an oil crisis or not?" We know by now that the answer is that this trading day is more likely to be a normal day, by around 11 chances to 1. Indeed, it is just comparing 99% of 1% to 10% of 99%. So, we have solved a classification problem – the two classes being *oil crisis days* and *normal days*.

106 9.9 / (9.9 + 99)

By computing the occurrences of particular evidence within the different classes – adjusted by the occurrence of these classes – and taking the maximum of these quantities, one can classify the sample. In other words, a *normal day* has a probability of 10% of having these words in the news, in a population size of 99% (normal days), which is superior to an *oil crisis day* having a probability of containing the words in 99% of the cases, in a population size of 1% (oil crisis days).

We could extend the analysis to other combinations of words and compute the same class probabilities. By assuming independence between the factors,[107] the class probability is just the product of all individual (marginal) probabilities. The highest probability, for the various possible classes, adjusted by the class prevalence, is the predicted class. In other words and in this specific example of a rare event, in order to be able to conclude that this event has a high chance of appearing, one needs to find a combination of words that are very unlikely on normal days but are very likely on crisis days.[108]

We have seen that, by computing these class (conditional) probabilities, we can build a non-linear classifier, thanks to Bayes' theorem. This classifier is actually in use in practice and is called *Naive Bayes*.[109] Given its simplicity, the model is computationally efficient on extensive datasets. In particular, it is implemented in text classification tasks, where documents – as collections of words – are classified into specific categories.

---

107 In practice, a (small) smoothing parameter is added, to avoid situations where the estimated probability is 0

108 This is exactly the problem faced by medical tests of rare diseases. The simple fact that healthy patients may still test positive makes even highly efficient tests difficult to use in practice

109 *Naive* because of the assumption of independence between features, which, even though unrealistic, works well in many practical cases

12

ALGORITHMS (PART 1): SUPERVISED LEARNING

"Though experience be our only guide in reasoning concerning matters of fact; it must be acknowledged, that this guide is not altogether infallible, but in some cases is apt to lead us into errors."

David Hume

The Elements of Statistical Learning[110] – a great early reference book about techniques in machine learning – has 764 pages. It only briefly touches on neural networks, ignores natural language processing altogether, and does not cover the last ten years of research. Ian Goodfellow and colleagues' book,[111] another excellent textbook on deep learning, is 800 pages long. So, how can I present the extended field of machine learning algorithms in just a few pages? It is definitely a challenge. But it is also so critical to understand machine learning at a deeper level that I cannot exclude the topic entirely.

Also, by design, this book does not include any maths. That makes the task of introducing models even harder. In most cases, a couple

110 (Friedman, Hastie and Tibshirani 2001)
111 (Goodfellow, Bengio and Courville 2016)

of equations would quickly convey the key ingredients. However, not only did I not want to put off the non-technical reader, but more crucially, it would have been a distraction if the intuition was obscured by the maths. I want the reader to develop a feeling and an intuitive understanding for the solutions, instead of paying too much attention to intellectual rigour.

Fortunately, one way to cut down on the model presentation is to ignore their implementation. For the most part, a task is solved by optimising an objective function. As a practical field of computer science, a large part of modern machine learning research is dedicated to concerns like optimisation efficiency, training speed, etc. The discipline of numerical optimisation is fertile. But thankfully, these methods are now quickly integrated into machine learning platforms by an army of – mostly volunteer – talented engineers and programmers. Solving some of the models can be very challenging indeed, but, as practitioners, we can leave this aside in the discovery phase.

ADVANCE WARNING

The below review may seem daunting at first. Given the breadth of the discipline, it might feel like a long litany of models. But, take a closer look, and you will realise that each of them has something unique. My selection process has been mostly about uncovering these particular attributes.

It might still take a few passes to digest the material. It is not for the faint-hearted, but if you stick to it, you will get much closer to a deeper understanding of how AI can achieve its goals.

Genuinely understanding machine learning requires that initial investment. Nobody would pretend to know an artist without seeing any of her masterpieces. Nevertheless, there is no need to rush. The key is for these concepts to slowly sink in.

Also, it is worth noting that there is no unified classification of machine learning algorithms. Models could be defined by their many dimensions, for instance their formulation, the problems they can solve, the theory behind them, or the implementation techniques they use. And, they usually belong to multiple categories at once. My presentation choice is driven by the aim of developing an intuition, but bear in mind that you may encounter different ways to group them.

A FIRST LOOK AT LINEAR MODELS

Let us first imagine that one wants to build a system that predicts market returns from its technical indicators, like a technical analyst would do. The set of inputs are a variety of indicators, typically, about momentum, volume and volatility. The output is the market performance at the next time step. It is a real-value output, so we are squarely within a *regression task* in *supervised learning*.

An obvious first choice is to linearly combine these indicators to form a prediction as close as possible to the *ground truth*. The weights in the mixture of inputs indicate the strength – or importance – of each indicator and its direction. For instance, a large positive weight signifies a meaningful positive factor to future returns. This makes these models *highly interpretable*, which is a reason for their popularity. The most obvious algorithm to achieve this is the well-known *linear regression*, better characterised as *Ordinary Least Squares* (OLS) regression. Geometrically, on a familiar 2D chart, it looks like a straight line minimising its distance to the data points.

NON-LINEARITY, FEATURE EXPLOSION, AND PARAMETERS UNCERTAINTY

An important limitation in OLS is its linearity. Indeed, the rate of response to any input change is constant across the range of input values. It means that the importance of a single variable is always the same, whatever the data sample that is considered. A doubling of an input value will have double the effect on the output. That is what most people think – and it is correct in the standard setting of OLS. But, that is not always true. Linearity in the model is not what you think. It means linearity *in the weights*, not in the variables themselves. So, one trick we can use is to expand the variables to their square, cube,[112] etc. It is called *polynomial expansion*. This way the response to a variable input does not need to be linear. It could take any polynomial form. For instance, beyond a certain value, the effect of a particular variable could be a lot less prevalent, which may well be the case in real life.

Solving that *expanded* problem is as inexpensive as the standard OLS. In short, OLS, contrary to popular belief, can handle non-linearity in its input variables. Even better, that *trick* can be extended to other functions,[113] not just polynomials. This technique can be linked to a more general technique, used across machine learning: the *kernel trick*. Thanks to a mathematical property,[114] it is computationally easy to expand the features to a richer higher dimensional space, and transform a linear model into a non-linear one.

So, the problem of non-linearity is solved by a standard OLS? Not so fast. What we can do with such a technique is solve for a particular form of non-linearity. It would not be possible to handle more complex effects. For instance, capturing something like "a *high momentum indicator & low volatility indicator* is conducive to high expected returns", but not other combinations, would be problematic. Also, there is no easy framework to know what *basis function*

---

112 As well as their cross products

113 This more general technique is called *basis expansion*

114 (Mercer's theorem 2020)

to use. And, finally it could lead to *feature explosion*, i.e. many more input variables to manipulate.

We know by now that too many features may be a problem in machine learning. This is where *parameter regularisation* comes into play. A *Ridge Regression* directly addresses the problem of overfitting, by reducing the importance of features that appear to have a disproportionate impact. A *LASSO Regression* attempts to drop unnecessary features. These two models are theoretically more satisfying and may generalise better.

But, what about weight estimation? OLS has a well-known closed-form solution, meaning that it can be computed exactly and cheaply. However, for the whole class of models I talked about, it is easier to think about solving them through learning. *Gradient descent* can iteratively minimise the objective function – typically, the distance between predictions and actual targets – by taking the shortest path to the minimum. But, how do we know that the solution is satisfying? We have the whole corpus of model testing, which estimates model quality in terms of generalisation error, etc.

But, in this debate, it is also useful to take a detour through two different perspectives on the field of machine learning. *Frequentists* and *Bayesians* have opposing views on what constitutes a good model. For the frequentists – the vast majority – what really matters is the quality of the predictions. There is nothing more to it than extracting information from the data. On the contrary, the Bayesians need to stipulate an intrinsic prior knowledge of the data distribution – that could, for instance, come from domain knowledge. The data collected is not the source of information per se, but instead is there to confirm that prior knowledge. Intuitively, as one gathers more data, one gets a better knowledge of the phenomenon at play, i.e. a better confidence in the model parameters. As an example, *Bayesian Linear Regression* does this. It looks like a standard linear regression, but the purpose is to update[115] the parameters distribution – *the prior* – with the data at hand. Having access to a distribution[116] – and not just an estimation – means that we can now quantify the quality of the parameters, and measure our confidence in the model.

A FIRST LOOK AT CLASSIFICATION

By combining features, we have solved typical regression tasks, or making real-valued predictions. What if we need to classify outputs in distinct classes, or categories? Let us start with a 2-class problem, or *binary classification*. For instance, in our chartist problem, instead of predicting market returns, we could just forecast their direction, *up* or *down*. An obvious way to achieve this is to reuse our linear regression model, and postulate that low predicted values mean *market down*, and high values *market up*. This is what a *Logistic Regression*[117] does.

It takes a real-value output – as a combination of features in a linear regression – and maps it to a [0,1] output. A candidate for such a mapping is the *sigmoid function* – or *logistic function*. It is a smooth function that takes any real number and transforms it into a value between 0 and 1. If it is close to 1, it will *classify* the sample as *class 0* – or *market down* in our trading example. The reverse will be the case for a predicted value close to 1. The primary advantage of choosing a 0-to-1 range is that the output is analogous to a probability. A sample with a prediction of 0.99 means that it has a very high chance of belonging to class 1 – and by opposition, a very low chance, of 0.01, of

---

115 It naturally uses the Bayes' theorem to do so

116 By opposition to drawing a distribution, a single estimate of an unknown parameter is called a *point estimate*

117 *Logistic Regression* is an unfortunate term, as *Logistic Regression* handles *classification* tasks, and not *regressions*

belonging to class 0. We just solved a market direction problem, but a classic use of this algorithm could be to forecast default probabilities in a credit risk task.

As a direct extension of linear regression to classification tasks, Logistic Regression is a very commonly used algorithm for practical business decisions. It is highly interpretable. For example, a feature with a high positive weight is meaningful for a class 1 prediction. It can also be extended to multiclass problems, beyond two classes. The mapping function would just take a different form, and is called a *softmax function*.[118]

Logistic Regression is part of a broader class of linear algorithms, which further expand their capabilities. *Generalised Linear Models* (GLMs) – popular in insurance underwriting, for instance – use a *link function*, to map the traditional linear combination of features to the desired output. In the case of a Logistic Regression, the link function is the sigmoid function, but in a *Poisson Regression*, it would be a *Poisson function*. The latter is employed to model rare occurrence events, for instance in risk management.

A GLIMPSE INTO NEURAL NETWORKS

Let us go back to the first neural classifier that was invented, the *Perceptron*. As a reminder, it was created by Frank Rosenblatt in 1958. It is a binary classifier and is even simpler than the logistic regression. What if, instead of using the S-curve sigmoid function, we had done something even simpler? If the output of a linear regression is below a certain threshold, it is classified as class 0, and above, as class 1. The link function is just a *step function*, with two states. That is a perfectly valid way to transform a regression problem into a classification problem.

118 The softmax function is a simple extension of the sigmoid function, and is widely used – including in neural networks – to map real value outputs to discrete classes

However, it is not used in practice, because of at least two issues. For classes that are not separable[119] – which is the case for real-life problems – the solution is not unique. Also, there is no way to make sure that the algorithm finds a good enough candidate amongst the infinity of solutions. From a machine learning theory standpoint, it is interesting because it shows – in a very simple example – the depth of the mathematical complications underpinning the field. A more straightforward model, the Perceptron, quickly becomes pathological. The reason is simple here. The step function is discontinuous (at the threshold level) and more difficult to handle than the smooth sigmoid function.

But, that is not my primary reason for mentioning the Perceptron. Like often in AI, there are different vantage points worth considering. There is indeed an interesting parallel with the functioning of the brain. The output of a Perceptron is analogous to how a neuron works. It processes inputs – the features – like a neuron takes input from the neurons connected to it. It learns *weights*, similarly to how *synapses* adjust the signal strength. And, if the combination of these inputs reaches a certain threshold, it outputs 1, akin to the *neuron firing*. So, a Perceptron unit looks close to how electrical signals are processed in the brain. This aspect was the inspiration for the initial Perceptron machine. At the time, the hope was that it could solve any type of problem – by analogy to the way the brain operates. It is no longer used in its current specification, but the same principles still apply in neural networks. A *feed-forward neural network* takes inputs from previous neurons and combines them to form an input to the next layer of neurons. The Perceptron is just the simplest form of such an artificial neuron network.

---

119 Think of it as a line that would neatly separate the two classes of data points on a 2D chart. That line in 2D is called a *hyperplane* in higher dimensions

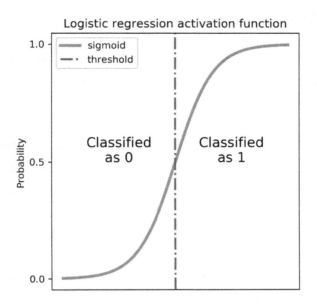

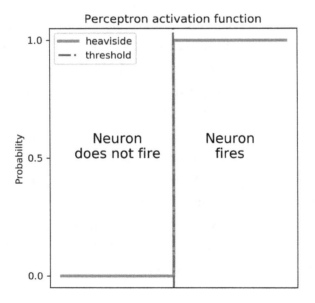

Figure 7 – Logistic Regression and Perceptron activation functions. Sigmoid and Heaviside step functions. We can observe the smooth activation curve in a Logistic Regression by opposition to the discontinuous one in a Perceptron.

BAYESIAN MODELLING

Let us now envision an investment banker interested in a machine that consumes news and company press releases to get an edge on identifying potential deal ideas. He is interested in a text classifier that instantaneously reads all incoming news and tags them with a specific category. For instance, he is not interested in following up on a piece that is flagged as "product release", but may want to reach out to his client if it says "financing transaction". We assume that one can access a dataset that contains these news categories – or labels – maybe from past analysed press stories. This does not need to be exhaustive, just relevant enough for the task at hand.

A *Naive Bayes Classifier* does this efficiently and very quickly, even on very large quantities of data. I talked about that type of classifier in a previous section, but I will remind you of the procedure. The first step,[120] like in most natural language processing tasks, is to compute the occurrence probability of each word in the vocabulary for every topic.[121] It is a simple counting exercise: how often has that particular word appeared in the set of documents for that category? For instance, "debt" would be relatively frequent in "financing transaction", but probably absent in "product release". The purpose is to compute the likelihood of seeing a particular word, given the context – or news category. The process is repeated for all possible words. The other piece of input is just the probability of each category, which is again a counting exercise of documents of a given category within the whole corpus. And, the two steps conclude the model training.

---

120 I will be making some simplifications in the methodology to just focus on the crucial steps

121 That is called *likelihood* in Bayesian inference, and represents the likelihood of seeing that word given the context

When presented with a new document, it is intuitive to understand that the machine is more likely to allocate it to a given category, say "financing transaction", than to others, in two situations. If, of course, that particular category is frequent. And also, if the words in the document are representative of that category, or, to put it differently, if their combined probability in the context of that topic is relatively high. Bayes' theorem tells us that only the product of these two quantities is required to assign the document to a category.

The only simplification in Naive Bayes is to treat each word independently from the others, and to therefore multiply all individual word probabilities. For instance, words like "debt", "equity", "acquisition", "capex", "synergies" are likely to have a high probability in the context of "financing transaction", compared to "product release". If a piece of news were to contain some or all of these words – and the category "financing transaction" were not too rare in the news feed – it is very likely it would be flagged as a "financing transaction".

In slightly more formal terms, the predicted class is the one that maximises the probability of the data given that class (*likelihood*) times the probability of that class (*prior*).[122] The former is the product of all individual conditional probabilities – as the model assumes (conditional) independence between the features (cf. *naive*). If the features are categorical, like in our text classification example, it leads to the *Categorical Naive Bayes* model, which estimates the likelihoods by their relative frequencies in the data.[123] If the likelihoods are assumed Gaussian, we can easily estimate their sets of parameters, and we talk about *Gaussian Naive Bayes*. The *Multinomial Naive Bayes* is the extension of the *Categorical Naive Bayes* to multinomial distributions and is estimated in the same manner.

---

122 Estimated by the relative frequency of the class

123 With a smoothing parameter to deal with nil frequencies

It is now easy to see the merits of Naive Bayes, compared to some other classifiers. It can deal with very high dimensionality – like the size of the vocabulary in a text classification task (thousands of dimensions). Also, conditional independence – of words, in our example – helps combat the curse of dimensionality. Otherwise, given the very high dimensionality, we would need to have a ridiculous amount of data to represent all possible combinations of features (words). This is one of the reasons why such models work well in practice for this type of task.

INSTANCE-BASED MODELS

Consider now an analyst on a desk that has been tasked with categorising new clients. There is an existing database with client groups, and all sorts of client attributes, like their industry, the products they trade, etc. How can we go about suggesting a client group for a client that is not already tagged? An intuitive answer is to classify that customer as the ones that look the most similar. The famous *Nearest Neighbors* algorithm exploits that simple idea. Firstly, one needs to transform that data into machine-readable data, which is as straightforward as organising that data in relevant data columns.[124] Then, it is just a question of defining a measure of *similarity*. It is usually a simple distance between data samples, like a *Euclidean distance*. The *closest* clients to the new customer can then be identified, and the new client is usually allocated to the majority category amongst these *neighbours*. We call it a *voting mechanism*, as each *neighbour* is voting for its own category and the majority wins.

124 For categorical data, like an industry, the standard method is called *one-hot encoding*. It creates as many columns as there are categories, and records a 1 in the *one* relevant column, and 0 elsewhere.

This can also easily be turned into a regression problem. If we are after a particular score for this client, we could simply take the mean of its neighbours' scores. This algorithm is used extensively in practice in supervised tasks, like classification and regression, but also in unsupervised learning, in clustering exercises or as part of a more complex pipeline. This is the simplest example of an *instance-based model* – also called *memory-based model*. This terminology emanates from the fact that these models compare new samples to *instances seen* in training (or stored in memory).

There are many variations of the algorithm implementation to deal with computational efficiency. Indeed, in its *brute-force* version, it requires many distances to be computed and therefore may not scale well with the training size. It also suffers from the curse of dimensionality, due to the possibly very large number of feature combinations. However, its non-parametric nature and its ability to learn irregular boundaries means it is adaptable to complex situations. It can identify complex frontiers between classes that some more constrained algorithms may never find.

Support Vector Machine (SVM) is another very capable and popular algorithm, for both classification and regression tasks. Despite its apparent simplicity, it has a solid mathematical foundation. The algorithm is a *maximum margin classifier*, in the sense that the objective is to find a *hyperplane*[125] that maximises the distance to the closest point in each class. In looser terms and for a binary classification problem, its goal is to place the frontier right in the middle of the two classes,[126] in order to properly separate the two classes and generalise well. The

---

125 A hyperplane, in geometry, is a part of the space whose dimension is one less than the space it lives in – like a line in a 2D space, or a plane in 3D

126 Of course, in real-world situations, classes are non-separable. The algorithm introduces *slack variables* in the objective function to allow for some misclassification, with some penalty

learning revolves around maximising the gap between the closest points in the respective classes.

The frontier may be linear, like a line in 2D, a plane in 3D. But, where it shines in practice is when used as a non-linear classifier to come up with more complex data structures. For instance, it can correctly identify doughnut-type shapes. To do so, it uses the *kernel trick*, to expand the problem into a higher dimensional – possibly infinite – space, where it can separate the classes more easily. This richer nature makes the algorithm a strong contender in a variety of concrete tasks.

DECISION TREES

In our market prediction task, we may want to guide the solution in a different way. Not as a bunch of inputs contributing at once to the output, but more in a sequential manner. The ultimate task is to predict whether the market is likely to go *up* or *down*. For instance, one might think that the most important *first* question is whether the market volatility is *high* or *low*. If the answer is *low*, the next question could be whether the momentum indicator is *high* or *low*. But if the answer is *high*, it might be about volume indicators. Tree-based models are a series of *if-then* questions, to ultimately create as uniform as possible clusters of data. At a leaf level – or commonly the bottom of the tree – these regions would be strongly associated with the market going *up* or *down*. Most importantly, questions may involve different variables on different branches, so these architectures can handle a high degree of *non-linearity*.

Tree-based models are similar to decision trees in expert systems, which encode human knowledge. However, here, the rules are learned directly from data, without any prior knowledge. The standard model is the *Classification and Regression Tree* (CART), which

Separatable classes and maximum margin

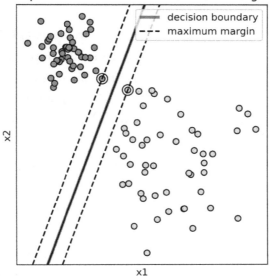

Decision boundaries for various kernels

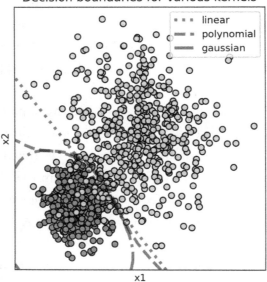

Figure 8 – SVM decision boundaries. Illustration of decision boundaries, maximum margin and use of kernel.

can handle both types of tasks. But, how does the learning mechanism work?

At each node of the tree (and starting from the *stump*), that region of data is split in two, according to a specific rule. Importantly, the *splitting rule* at each node answers a question about a *single* feature only. For a continuous variable, it is whether that variable is below or above a certain threshold. For a categorical variable, it is whether that variable is of a specific category. To grow a tree, the algorithm looks for the splitting rule that is the *most informative* across all features. For instance, it was the *volatility* at the start of our imaginary tree. Most *informative* means that, after a split, the two newly created regions have the lowest *classification error*.[127] As the tree is grown, purer and purer areas appear, up until the tree is stopped. At a leaf-node, the majority class is returned as prediction – or the mean value in a regression task.

Trees have many advantages. They are *non-parametric* and therefore versatile. They are easy to interpret and represent. They can handle all sorts of data, and they require little data preparation. Making a prediction is as easy as reading the tree from top to bottom and answering the question at each *node*, to get to the prediction at a *leaf-node*.

The recursive splitting rule is powerful to learn complex and non-linear rules. The flip side is that trees are prone to overfitting. Also, they come with many hyperparameters that need to be tuned.[128] The most crucial one to reduce overfitting is the maximum tree depth.[129] As a result of overfitting, trees may be unstable when presented with slight variations in the input data, i.e. a sign of *high variance*.

127 Beyond the classification error, the *gini index* or *entropy* can be used as a measure of quality

128 For instance, the minimum number of samples required to split a node – or at a leaf-node – or the minimum impurity decrease to allow a split

129 There are also other techniques to prune back a fully grown tree

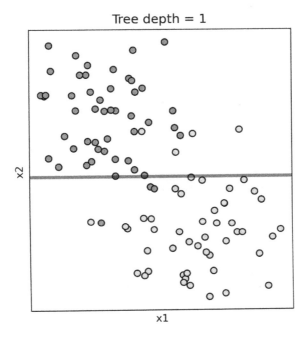

Tree depth = 1

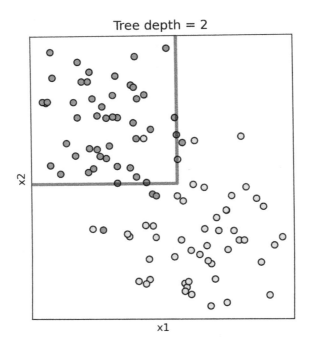

Tree depth = 2

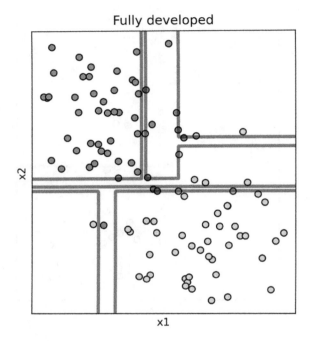

Figure 9 – illustration of possible overfitting in trees.
Possible overfitting in trees, as controlled by maximum
tree depth. Note the boundaries perpendicular to the
axes, a characteristic of decision trees.

ENSEMBLE LEARNING

So, how do we solve the issue of overfitting in individual trees? The answer is in the question. We combine many of them. This is the broad idea behind *ensemble models*. The idea is to build multiple models (ideally as decorrelated as possible), enquire about their individual predictions, and then aggregate these predictions through a voting mechanism, or similar mechanism. This technique describes what is often called a *Voting Classifier*.

Behind the concept of *ensemble learning* is an effective idea, akin to the wisdom of the crowd, whereby a collection of similar models are combined to produce superior predictions. One example of such a combination is called *bagging* (for *bootstrap aggregating*). In the *bootstrapping* step, the algorithm draws m sets of n samples – with replacement – from the original data (of size n). It then trains m individual trees and aggregates their predictions into a single one, through voting, or an equivalent procedure.

This simple procedure of training on multiple sets of data reduces variance and helps create a much stronger learner. However, the trees remain somewhat correlated, and the benefit is not maximised. A simple variation is to also randomly use only a subset of features for each bootstrapped tree. In doing so, the benefit of ensemble learning is maximal. This is the famous *Random Forest* algorithm, which regularly figures in the leaderboard of best supervised learning algorithms. The success of the Random Forest algorithm comes from its two sources of randomness: selecting random training samples and random features for each tree.

Another approach in ensemble learning is to build *sequential* trees in a procedure called *boosting*. Robert E. Schapire and Yoav Freund made this colourful comment in their seminal book about boosting: "How is it that a committee of blockheads can somehow arrive at highly reasoned decisions, despite the weak judgment of the individual members?"[130] Surprisingly, *weak learners* – doing not much better than random guessing – like shallow trees, when combined, are able to reduce bias meaningfully. The model introduced by Schapire and Freund is called *AdaBoost*. The algorithm builds successive trees that are forced to focus on *errors* made by the previous tree. It does so by increasing the weights on the wrongly predicted training samples –

130 (Schapire and Freund 2012)

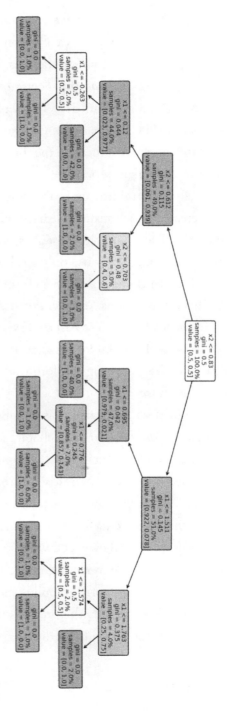

Figure 10 - splitting rules for a fully developed decision tree

and lowering the weights on correctly predicted samples – to itera-tively improve predictions.

Another very effective version of boosting is called *Gradient Boost-ing*. Similarly to AdaBoost, the algorithm builds consecutive trees, which focus on errors made by the previous tree. However, this time, the trees are no longer averaged at the end, but their predictions added up. Indeed, each tree is constructed to better predict the *residual errors* made by the preceding tree. The popularity of Gradient Boosting has led to many implementations of the algorithm to achieve increased performance from a computational standpoint. For example, *XGBoost* brings several algorithmic improvements, and regularly competes with some of the most advanced architectures in neural networks.

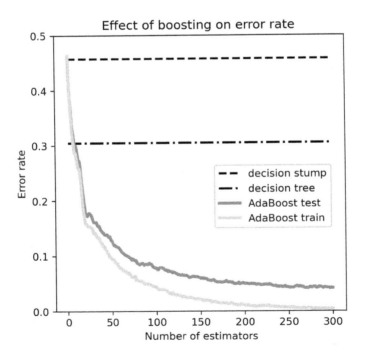

Figure 11 – illustration of the benefit of boosting. Benefit of boosting versus a single decision tree (and a 1-level tree – or stump).

For supervised learning tasks in finance, Random Forest and Gradient Boosting are the workhorses of machine learning models. They combine the power of *trees* on complex data with *ensemble learning* to dramatically improve model performance.

13

ALGORITHMS (PART 2): UNSUPERVISED LEARNING

"It is wrong to think that the task of physics is to find out how Nature is. Physics concerns what we can say about Nature."

Niels Bohr

Most tasks in machine learning use supervised learning. Yet, most of the data produced around us comes unlabelled – the data samples are untagged. This is unlikely to change, as categorising data has a cost associated with it. Somebody needs to do it. So, the next frontier in AI is to make more extensive usage of unlabelled data. It means finding patterns or structure in the data that the machine has not been directed to do, and for which there is no *ground truth*.

The reason why one can be hopeful in such tasks is that nature is highly structured.[131] Not all combinations of features exist in the real world. And undoubtedly, they do not have the same probability of occurrence. In other words, randomness is difficult to find in this highly ordered natural world. I usually take the example of an image made of pixels. Even at low resolutions, the likelihood

---

131 Its structure is even hierarchical, from the atom to the universe

of randomly selected pixels forming a recognisable picture is close to 0.

In short, we should expect to find a structure in unstructured data. And there are tools for it, which is the purpose of the chapter. These are established techniques that are commonly used, but we can hope for many more discoveries in the field in the medium-term future.

CLUSTERING MODELS

Within unsupervised learning, clustering is a generic and widely used method that attempts to reveal structure in *unlabelled* data by grouping samples that have some level of similarity. In finance, the applications are numerous, like clustering clients' profiles, clients' behaviours, securities, or any other type of data that contains a hidden order.

For example, to understand the current market environment at a macro level it could be informative to imagine possible future developments or upcoming risks. After all, history in markets tends to repeat itself. Equipped with a broad selection of market and economic indicators, one could attempt to organise these into relatively homogeneous categories. We might not be able to label these groups, but they might still exist. Identifying market regimes is a typical use of clustering. For example, clustering clients according to profiles and patterns of activity is a well-known use case for salespeople. It is often utilised as a preliminary step to other tasks, like reorganising client coverage, or making more tailored product or service recommendations.

K-Means is the most intuitive clustering algorithm and is an iterative process to form K disjoint *clusters* of data points. Each cluster contains data points that minimise the distance to the centre of the cluster (*centroid*). At each iteration, centroids are updated to be slowly positioned right in the centre of its cluster. The algorithm scales well to large datasets, hence its popularity. However, given the distance used,[132] it works best with particular shapes of clustered data, mostly regular blob shapes (or in mathematical terms, *convex*[133] and *isotropic*[134]). Also, given the curse of dimensionality and distances exploding with dimensionality, it might be necessary to use a *dimensionality reduction* technique first.

Gaussian Mixture Model (GMM) could be seen as an extension of K-Means. It is a bit more involved mathematically, but in simple words, it assumes that the data is generated by a combination (*mixture*) of (Gaussian) distributions. Given its probabilistic nature, one option is to use Bayesian inference to estimate its parameters. Crucially, the richness of the model allows the identification of less regular cluster shapes, in particular elongated clusters, with different orientations. Also, GMM is a *soft clustering*[135] mechanism: it returns a set of probabilities of belonging to the various clusters, and not just to one cluster like in K-Means. This provides a more satisfactory output as some data points might be best described as belonging to two or more clusters.

The very popular *Density-Based Spatial Clustering of Applications with Noise* (usually, known as DBSCAN) seeks to address some limitations of K-means too. It sees the data space as regions of *high density* (clusters), separated by areas of *low density* (outliers or noise). High-density regions regroup points (*core samples*) with numerous neighbours, i.e. points that fall below a certain distance threshold. Points that are far from their neighbours are *outliers*. DBSCAN is superior to K-Means in many respects. It can recover many cluster

---

132 Various distance definitions may be used, but it is commonly the Euclidean distance

133 Which contains all segments that join two points

134 Whose geometry is the same regardless of direction

135 Also called *fuzzy clustering*

shapes, and there is no need to specify *a priori* the number of clusters. It is also robust to outliers.

Sometimes, as in nature itself, a data structure exists in a hierarchical sense. *Hierarchical Clustering*, as its name indicates, builds nested clusters by progressively merging (bottom-up) or splitting (top-down) existing clusters. It is best visualised in a *dendrogram* and is useful for analysing data with some embedded hierarchy in it. For instance – without prior knowledge – it could retrieve the path going from a whole equity market to individual stocks, by going through sectors, sub-sectors, etc. It may also be used as a complement to basic correlation analysis for portfolio construction. One strategy, for a bottom-up approach (called *agglomerative*), is to recursively merge pairs of clusters that minimally increase a given distance. The most similar clusters are iteratively grouped together to reveal a higher order.

Spectral Clustering is an interesting application, used in graph analysis, in particular. Graphs might have a complex hidden structure. Clusters might not look well-behaved, with data points smoothly grouped around distinct centres. To the human eye, clusters might be better organised using different shapes or might even be overlapping. Spectral Clustering involves three steps: defining a *similarity matrix*, reducing the dimensionality of the matrix, and then clustering by K-Means. The matrix similarity could be the existing connections in a graph (*edges* connecting *vertices*), or just the inverse of a distance (in a fully connected graph). The dimensionality reduction helps to form clusters of connected points which could be far away as assessed by a basic distance measure. In short, Spectral Clustering is able to retrieve a more elaborate data structure, and to also work on partially connected graphs.

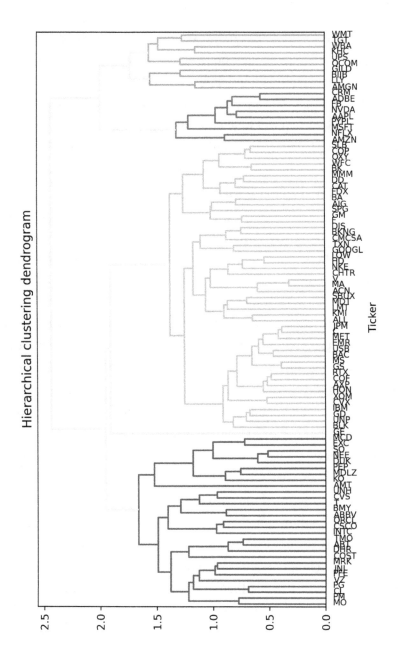

Figure 12 – example of a dendrogram for selected US stocks

DIMENSIONALITY REDUCTION

As soon as a piece of data has many attributes, we enter *high dimensionality* (one attribute of a data point is one dimension in space). On one level, dimensionality is good. It means that the business process is able to collect various relevant pieces of data. However, that brings its own complications – possibly issues with the curse of dimensionality, but also complexity and difficulty in visualising or making sense of that data. This is related to my point on big data. Richer data is in itself useful, but it requires building the appropriate techniques. One of them is the need to reduce the dimensionality of the data to achieve a better understanding.

Given the data overload in finance, dimensionality reduction techniques are commonly used in many concrete applications. They are often used in data preparation to reduce the problem to a smaller number of dimensions to improve model performance. Credit scoring and return predictions commonly use this in a preparatory phase. The methods may also be used on a standalone basis, for example, when analysing term structures of rates or volatilities. More recently, natural language processing, given the very high dimensionality of our vocabulary, has exploited such tools too.

A fertile field of linear algebra is *matrix factorisation*. As we observed, data is usually arranged in the form of matrices. Such a matrix can be decomposed into various types of products of matrices (the *components*), whose role is to extract the signal from the noise. The intention is to preserve as much of the value in the original data as possible while removing the noise. A well-known technique is the *Principal Component Analysis* (PCA). In this algorithm, the high dimensionality dataset is projected to a smaller space in order of decreasing importance. The first *component* explains most of the data,[136] the second most of the remainder, etc. The components are orthogonal directions in the new projection space and are just linear combinations of the original dimensions. One can then decide to keep as many components as necessary and reduce the signal to its main characteristics. This is a simple method that can be effective in the presence of correlated features or somehow redundant information. It can, therefore, be used as an extraction feature mechanism at the start of a machine learning problem.

Another algorithm of matrix factorisation, called *Non-Negative Matrix Factorisation* (NMF), uses a different, but intuitive technique. Instead of perfectly decomposing the input matrix, it solves for an approximate decomposition. The purpose of the algorithm is to minimise the difference between the original matrix and its decomposition.[137] With this general technique, we can force the components of the decomposition to have specific properties and control for the difference between the original and the reproduced matrix. NMF applies specifically to matrices with *non-negative* elements (both the input and the components). Applications could be in text processing – the matrix elements being the *term-document frequencies*[138] – or in cases where we have ratings or scores as inputs. In NMF, the dimensions (or *rank*) of the two components are much lower than the original dimensions, thereby forcing a more compact representation of the data, and extracting structure.

The concept of *rank* is an important one. It represents the dimensionality of the signal. The rest of the input data is just noise. For instance, when dealing with a thousand different clients, it could be that there are ten types of clients, but certainly not a thousand. Cli-

---

136 Or, more accurately, most of its variance

137 Usually using the Frobenius norm, which is the squared sum of the Euclidean distance, taken elementwise in a matrix

138 This is simply a record of the frequency of a term in a document

ents have some similarity, and that rank is just specifying that number of groups.

The *Latent Dirichlet Allocation* (LDA) is another way to extract hidden structure in the data through matrix factorisation. This time it is a probabilistic model, and it is often presented as building a *distribution of distributions*. It can be used in the same circumstances as NMF, but for ease of presentation, I will introduce it in the context of topic modelling for text objects, which is a popular application of the model. In this setting, we have a corpus of documents that we would like to organise into topics. The topics are unknown and are the expression of the (*latent*) structure that we are looking for. The modelling assumes that documents belong to a mixture of topics, the topics being themselves a collection of words. Documents are therefore represented as a distribution over topics, and topics as distributions over words, hence the term *distribution of distributions*.[139] The *document-term matrix* is decomposed into two smaller matrices, a *document-topic matrix* and a *topic-term matrix*, which are learned iteratively. It is worth noting that the topics here have some intuitive meaning – like a category of documents – but in general, understanding this intermediary step is not the goal. It is just a means to extract the structure within the input data.

In our lives, we have never visualised high dimensionality datasets, given our inability to see beyond 3D. Dimensionality reduction techniques may also be used for visualisation purposes, to project a complex dataset to a 2D or 3D space. The *t-distributed Stochastic Neighbor Embedding* algorithm (better known as t-SNE) does just that. Interestingly, t-SNE builds two distributions, in high dimensionality space and low dimensionality space respectively, in such a way that two similar data points are associated with a high proba-

---

139 Both being *Dirichlet distributions*

bility – and two dissimilar points with a low probability. It then uses a well-known metric to minimise the divergence between these two distributions, to preserve as much of the original similarity in a lower-dimensional space. In simple terms, it seeks to answer the question: how does one represent the structure of a high dimensionality problem in a low dimension in the most visually satisfying way?[140]

Finally, *Autoencoders* are a type of artificial neural network, used in many modern applications of AI – including to understand the semantic meaning of words. The two components in the network are an *encoder* which attempts to represent (*encode*) the input as a smaller hidden layer (*code*), and a *decoder* which reconstructs (*decodes*), from the code, an output to be as close as possible to the input. By forcing the network to retrieve as much of the input after compression, the intention is to remove the noise from the input data and extract its intrinsic structure. One pitfall to avoid is to constrain the network in such a way that it does not just learn the *identity function* – the perfect match between input and output – and instead learns richer representations. Researchers have developed many ingenious architectures to address this problem.

ANOMALY DETECTION

Another practical area of interest in data analysis is the detection of *anomalies* or abnormal observations. One domain is *outlier detection*, which attempts to identify *outliers* in the data, by opposing them to *inliers*. It is a technique often used for *data cleaning* or *data validation*, which are crucial for the performance of machine learning. Another field is *novelty detection*, which tries to predict

---

140 More specifically, t-SNE addresses the *crowding problem* – where nearby points are squashed together when represented in low dimension – with a *Student's t-distribution* (*t* in *t-SNE*)

Input   Output

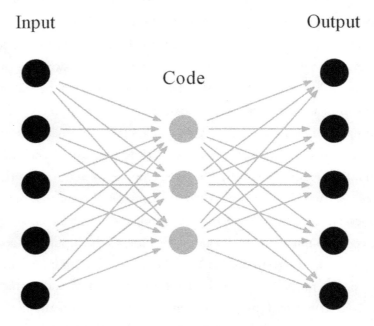

*Figure 13 – basic architecture of an Autoencoder. Note the
same size of the input and output, the goal being for the
output to be as close as possible to the input.*

whether a new data point differs from the training data, considered to be *normal*. One concrete application that comes to mind in
finance is fraud detection or the identification of other rare events.
In more statistical terms, the goal is to measure the likelihood that
a new transaction has been generated by the learned model which
describes standard transactions.

I will now make a quick digression. Anomaly detection sits across
supervised and unsupervised learning. Indeed, one could record,
once known, abnormal transactions and train a binary classifier
to identify such transactions. That would be a supervised learning

task. However, given the low occurrence of such abnormal transactions, the model might struggle to perform well. Another way is, in an unsupervised setting, to let the model figure out which transactions might sit outside what constitutes the bulk of observations, i.e. *normal* transactions. As indicated, it is commonly used in fraud detection, cybersecurity or market surveillance. Another use case is in market operations, to prevent failed settlements. Trained on a very large number of transactions, the machine identifies *outliers by itself* on the basis of combinations of factors that look abnormal. Such a task would be tedious for a human being. But a machine might easily pick up a missing entity in the transaction record, or two columns that surprisingly do not match, or an unusual transaction size, all things that could be associated with a failed settlement later down the chain.

As a field sitting across supervised and unsupervised learning, anomaly detection is particularly prolific. I will focus on three popular algorithms that demonstrate the versatility of approaches.

In the context of supervised learning, we came across the SVM model, in particular, when used with non-linear kernels. It is an algorithm that builds a frontier to separate classes with *maximum margin*. Here, we apply the same principle to a so-called *One-Class SVM*. Used for anomaly detection, the model draws a frontier around the contour of the normal distribution of points. If a new instance falls within the learned region, it is considered as usual, and if outside, as an outlier.[141]

Contrary to the previous algorithm that attempts to define normality, *Isolation Forest* focuses on *abnormal* points and tries to isolate them. It builds a collection of randomly generated trees. The idea is to

---

141 The algorithm needs to incorporate a tolerance for the possibility of normal data points sitting outside the frontier

randomly select *splitting rules* (feature and value) and recursively build trees to isolate every single data point. The interesting observation here is that the path to an outlier is noticeably shorter. Outliers are indeed rare and unusual, so they are easier to *isolate* in a tree. By recording the path length averaged over several trees, it becomes possible to identify anomalies, as the ones corresponding to the shorter paths.

The third technique is also based on a completely different approach. *Local Outlier Factor* (LOF) is quite intuitive. It is developed on the concept that outliers sit in regions of low density. LOF computes a score for each point that compares the density of the data point to the average density of its neighbours. *Normal* points will have a density similar to their (k-nearest) neighbours, whereas an *anomaly* will correspond to a much lower relative density.

In summary, unsupervised learning tries to find structure in data through a number of techniques – clustering, dimensionality reduction, or anomaly detection. There are other areas that I did not cover much, like *graph networks*. But, more fundamentally, the entire field is a prolific area of research, where we can expect much progress in the years to come. After all, even though most data comes unlabelled, we can still extract a lot of value from such data.

14

ALGORITHMS (PART 3): ARTIFICIAL NEURAL NETWORKS AND DEEP LEARNING

"Reason is immortal, all else mortal."
Pythagoras

Since the failures of symbolic AI in the 1990s, and most noticeably in the past 10 years, *artificial neural networks* (ANNs) have conquered AI. In my opinion, the reasons are three-fold. Firstly, computational power is of crucial importance in training ANNs – given their very large number of parameters compared to more traditional machine learning models. This was not available earlier. Secondly, they need a lot of data to be trained on, which we now have access to. This is due to the way they learn, and in particular, because they have very few specifications. They require many samples to gradually learn the key characteristics in the data. Lastly, they are very versatile. Fairly standard architectures can be used to solve a wide range of tasks, which is useful in practice. It means that they do not require much guidance. With sufficient resources and data, they truly learn by themselves with almost no prior human intervention.

Due to the breadth of coverage of the technology, it is difficult to summarise it in a few pages. Network architectures have been developed to solve the traditional tasks of machine learning, like classification, regression, dimensionality reduction, anomaly detection, etc. But they have also extended their reach to more complex problems, for instance computer vision and language understanding. It is impossible to review all possible architectures, but segmenting them by their key characteristics should be sufficient for a broad understanding.

We have encountered the Perceptron, which was an early version of a network. It resembles the typical building block of modern architectures. At a basic level, a neural network is trying to learn a function *transforming* an input into an output. The elementary units, the *neurons*, receive a signal from other neurons, process it and produce a transformed output that feeds other neurons. Neurons are organised into sequential layers, which can be thought of as capturing different levels of complexity in the data. *Deep learning* (DL) is the sub-field that builds deep networks, i.e. containing multiple layers. Practically, it is now used interchangeably with *neural networks*.

At the core of ANNs is the realisation that phenomena in our human experience or nature are profoundly hierarchical, and networks organised in successive layers should be able to capture this hierarchy.[142] On a more mathematical level, the *universal approximation theorem*[143] stipulates that any continuous function – the one transforming inputs to an output – can be approximated by an artificial neural network[144] at any level of accuracy. These two points may explain why ANNs can achieve incredible results with fairly simple architectures.

142 (Lin, Tegmark and Rolnick 2017)

143 (Pinkus 1999)

144 The universal approximation theorem is theoretical and does not comment on network topology or number of neurons to use

BASIC ARCHITECTURE

The simplest network architecture is the *Multilayer Perceptron* (MLP), which is, loosely speaking, an extension of the Perceptron. It is in the class of the *feed-forward neural networks*, meaning that the signal flows in one direction only, without any cycle. The network has an input and an output, with one or multiple *hidden layers* in between, composed of *neurons*. A neuron sums up the signals from connected neurons before transforming them through a *non-linear activation function*. The activation function could be of multiple forms but always has the ability to modulate the output – including to block it altogether for some functions. This particular network is called *fully connected*, as all neurons in the previous layer are connected to all neurons in the current layer – hence the large number of parameters. A parameter in such a network is the weight – or strength – of a connection between two neurons.

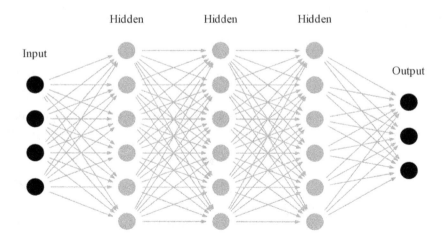

Figure 14 – architecture of an MLP

The learning mechanism – which solves for the weights attached to each connection – is through gradient descent in an algorithm called *backpropagation*. It propagates *backwards* the prediction error along the network.[145] For example, let us assume the task is a classification. If, during training, the class is wrongly predicted for a given sample, the backpropagation algorithm will reduce the weights of the connections that were the most activated in relation to that incorrect prediction. Over time, the weights will converge towards the optimal solution to maximise prediction accuracy.

It is worth noting the sheer size of the parameters for a fully connected network. For example, with an input size of 256, two hidden layers of 64 and 32 neurons respectively, and an output size of 10 neurons, the model needs to learn 18,858[146] parameters! That is a lot more than in a traditional linear regression, with its 257[147] parameters. And that would still be a fairly simple task, for instance classifying 16x16 grayscale pixel digit images in 10 classes, from 0 to 9. In computer vision, some networks have hundreds of layers, and parameter numbers can easily be in the millions.[148]

MLPs are very versatile and can be used to solve standard classification and regression problems. Note that, compared to their traditional machine learning cousins, there is no feature engineering step. The idea is that the network – through its layers and neurons – will perform *feature extraction* by itself, figuring out how inputs should be combined to produce the desired output. This is a fairly widespread result for ANNs. The network retrieves the data charac-

---

145 Using the chain rule used when computing derivatives

146 (256+1)x64 + (64+1)x32 + (32+1)x10, the +1 counting the bias term, like in a typical linear regression

147 256 (number of features) + 1 to account for the bias term

148 The language model, GPT-3, released by OpenAI in 2020, has 175 billion parameters

teristics worth learning for the particular task without being guided. The engineer only focuses on the optimal architecture, for instance trying different neural depth and granularity, but not on designing the particular features for the task.

This advantage of needing little guidance is also their main drawback. MLPs – and neural networks in general – are seen as black-boxes. There are techniques to help understand their behaviour, as I covered previously, but knowing their topology is not sufficient. One can comprehend *how* they learn, but much less *what* they learn. MLPs also require a lot of data for training – or pre-training. This may, or may not, be a problem. Even though it may constitute a major obstacle for some finance applications, in the case of textual data, for instance, there is usually an abundance of it. One technique is to use another text corpus to *pre-train* a model and use its parameters for the particular task at hand.

COMPUTER VISION

Convolutional Neural Networks (CNNs) are, without doubt, the most famous manifestation of deep learning in our daily lives. They handle image processing, from simple image classification to advanced computer vision in autonomous objects. For instance, in scene identification performed by modern cameras, CNNs have exceeded human performance. Also, their specific architecture to extract useful patterns may find applications in time series predictions too, and even language models.

The core concept is that images have an intrinsic structure. They are not just a collection of random pixels. Actually, if you think about it, the probability of getting a recognisable image by randomly colouring pixels is incredibly small, indistinguishable from 0.[149] Better, images have

---

149 The number of possible – very small – 16x16 pixel (256 pixels), monochromatic images is already of the order of magnitude ($2**256$ = c. $10**77$) of the number of atoms in the universe (c. $10**80$)

a hierarchical structure, edges and contours, then lines and shapes, and then forms and objects. To perform image recognition, networks have many layers, trying to capture increasingly higher-level features, as the signal processes through the network.

Similarly to the human visual cortex, CNNs use *local receptive fields*, which are small filters (for instance, 3x3 squares) that take as inputs a sub-area of the previous layer only. This technique of applying a filter to a part of the input is called a *convolution* – hence the name *Convolutional Neural Networks*. That dramatically reduces the number of parameters to learn, and enables the network to discover patterns. In contrast, a fully connected network – as in the case of MLPs – would have an incredible number of parameters to train, as all neurons are connected to all neurons in the previous layer.

Let us take a quick detour to understand how such an architecture works. In the first layer, it is easy to picture a filter scanning the whole image with a receptive field of 3x3 pixels, so that it focuses on very small areas of the picture at a time. Mathematically, these filters are represented by a matrix of weights – called a *kernel* – that apply to individual pixels in the 3x3 square. For instance, if the matrix was made of uniform weights, the application of the filter would return the average colour intensity in the square. Instead, if one uses weights that are organised in a certain vertical pattern,[150] the filter can recognise vertical edges in the image. Therefore, by using simple 3x3 pixel operations on the original image, one can perform *edge detection*.

But, this is not where the magic of CNNs happens. These operations are well-known image processing techniques. Where it is really surprising is that CNNs learn these methods on their own. No one is tediously implementing these filters, to recognise edges, then to

150 Sobel kernels are common for this: the vertical kernel is [[1,0,-1],[2,0,-2],[[1,0,-1]], and its transpose for the horizontal kernel. Note that, when applied to the area, they approximate the first order derivative along the two axes.

combine them into a higher order, etc. The algorithm learns these representations by itself. It turns out that, after being trained, CNNs exhibit these edge detection kernels in the first layer. In other words, without having been taught anything, CNNs recognise that detecting contours is the first of the most useful operations to perform on an image. They then repeat the concept to extract higher-order representations, like lines and shapes.

In finance, CNNs are being tried in tasks where this filter technology might be useful, for instance in modelling time series. Also, grouping words together through 1D convolutions can be useful for understanding a particular context in a corpus of documents. Closer to the cutting edge, image processing is being experimented on trading price representations – like candlesticks or price chart patterns – to predict future market performance. Lastly, it is extensively used in image satellite applications, in particular to measure economic activity.

HANDLING SEQUENTIAL DATA

There is often a temporal element in datasets in finance, for instance in the form of time series. *Recurrent Neural Networks* (RNNs) have been created to handle these cases, and, in general, sequences of data, where the order in the data matters – think temporal data or word order in texts. RNNs look similar to MLPs. But, they also have the ability to keep some memory of the previous steps, by incorporating *feedback loops* or *cycles* in the network. Neurons now receive signals from the previous layer, but also from the outputs at the previous time step. Getting inputs from the previous periods is a form of *memory*. By contrast, MLPs only take into account their current input, so they cannot remember previous sequences. That is obviously a problem in time-series where it is likely that phenomena have a certain permanency over time. Thanks to these cycles, RNNs contain *memory cells*.

Original image

Vertical edge detection

Horizontal edge detection

Figure 15 – example of kernel applications for edge detection. 3x3 Sobel kernels are used here.

However, this mechanism only exhibits short-term memory. The impact of past outputs quickly vanishes after a few time steps. To model longer-term dependencies, one needs a more sophisticated architecture. *Long Short-Term Memory* (LSTM) is such an advanced model network. Beyond remembering, it has the ability to *forget* too, hence the concept of *long short-term memory*. LSTMs are, in particular, the workhorse of language models. The context can usually be understood only if one can remember what has been said much earlier in the text. As linguist John Rupert Firth put it, "you shall know a word by the company it keeps".

GENERATING NEW DATA

We have covered Autoencoders previously in the context of dimensionality reduction. *Variational Autoencoders* have a similar architecture but are a *generative model*. Their aim is to *generate* synthetic *new* data, after having learned compressed representations of the initial data through an encoder.

But in the field of generative models, *Generative Adversarial Networks* (GANs) are the gold standard. Their architecture is ingenious, as it involves two competing networks,[151] a *generator* and a *discriminator*. The *generator* is the *counterfeiter* and tries to generate data samples that resemble the training data as closely as possible. The *discriminator* is the *expert*, and its function is to distinguish the fake samples from the true samples coming from the training data itself. As the training progresses, both the generator and the discriminator get better at their job. Ultimately, the generator becomes able to create samples quasi-indistinguishable from the real data.

There are many applications of such networks, including the

---

151 Hence the term *adversarial* in *Generative Adversarial Network*

famous *deepfakes*.[152] But, in finance, where data quantity may be an issue, there are high hopes that GANs will be able to produce new samples that closely mimic reality, in the form of *synthetic datasets*. In trading, it would be like creating imaginary trading days indiscernible from the real ones. This technology could dramatically strengthen the idea of *back-testing* investment strategies by testing ideas on more extensive market configurations.

152 For instance, a GAN is behind the generation of realistic but imaginary faces: (This person does not exist n.d.)

15

ALGORITHMS (PART 4): NATURAL LANGUAGE PROCESSING

"Language is a system of signs that express ideas."

Ferdinand de Saussure

Natural language processing (NLP) is a vast field in itself. *Natural* stands for human, as opposed to computer, language. NLP does not constitute a completely separate area of machine learning. In many concrete cases, it is just a question of representing textual data as the first part of a machine learning pipeline. That comment particularly applies to subjects of interest to us in finance, mostly around understanding, in a broad sense, documents. There are other valuable tasks within NLP, like *machine translation* or *speech recognition*, but they are not specific to finance. Note that, in these complex cases, it is likely that the superior architecture is some form of RNNs handling *sequence-to-sequence*[153] architecture.

---

153 *Sequence* here typically refers to a group of words or sentences

MACHINE LANGUAGE

In English, texts come in the form of letters, words and sentences. These are not the typical inputs of a machine learning model – with a view to classifying documents, for instance. Therefore, the first part of the pipeline requires that we map words, for example, to real-valued inputs, which can then be understood by the algorithm. This step is called *vectorisation*. The most basic technique is a *Bag-of-Words* (BoW). It is simply counting the occurrences of individual words (collectively called a *vocabulary*) within a document, and creating a vector of these occurrences (0 meaning the word is absent in the document). As you can see, it ignores grammar, word positions, etc., but it works well in many applications. A more advanced variation is the *Term Frequency-Inverse Document Frequency*, or more commonly, *TF-IDF*. It computes the frequency of a word in a document, but also inversely adjusts it by the frequency of the word across documents. It is trying to capture words that are relevant for the specific document, as opposed to being just frequent across the corpus.

LANGUAGE COMPLEXITY AND SEMANTICS

If vectorisation is required for machines to consume text, other hurdles exist in human language. They revolve around two areas: *syntax* – including grammar – and *semantics*. Syntax has to do with the intricacy of our language, whether it is the way we form words or the way we create sentences. Techniques like *lemmatisation* (the dictionary form of a word[154]) and *stemming* (a word's root[155]) help with grouping words ultimately representing the same term. *Part-of-*

154 *Best* would be replaced with *good*
155 *Learning* would be replaced with *learn*

speech tagging (the category of a word, like a *noun, verb, adjective*) and *parsing* (grammatical analysis, like the relationship between words) address the issue of constructing sentences.

But, without doubt, the more significant challenge – which resembles more traits associated with real intelligence – is *semantics*. The issue of *meaning*, especially within a particular context or discipline, is an intricate one. For instance, *sentiment analysis* is an attempt to understand the tone of a document. *Word sense disambiguation* is tasked with avoiding understanding a word in the wrong context.[156] *Relationship extraction* is about the relationship between words in a given sentence. *Named-entity recognition* tries to automatically tag places, persons, organisations, locations, etc, which is useful in text classification, for example. All these tools are an effort to get closer to the true sense that machines cannot *naturally* apprehend.

NEURAL APPROACH AND WORD EMBEDDINGS

In the past decade, neural approaches have emerged to better represent an entire vocabulary and extract more relevant meaning than just a statistical description would do. Indeed, in traditional machine learning techniques, *meaning* derives primarily from the *co-occurrence* of certain words. Certain terms appearing together must somehow carry some information, or reveal a particular context.

Natural approaches try to go beyond simple distributions of words, and more formally unearth a particular context through training. The good news is that textual data is ubiquitous, and therefore offers a great training ground for language models. For instance, it is not uncommon to train models on repositories like the entire corpus of Wikipedia pages – with billions of words.

---

156 For instance, *bond* has a particular meaning in finance

Extracting such representations in textual data is called *embeddings*, and in our specific setting, *word embeddings*. As I have explained previously, word vectorisation implies the modelling of documents by very sparse vectors of the length of the entire vocabulary. Also, if you think about it, in that representation, each word sits alongside a single axis, alone, in a very high dimensionality space – typically, thousands of dimensions. It does not seem optimal. Ideally, to have a better understanding of word meanings – as data points in a space – we would like to have words appearing closer together in that space when they have similar meaning. *Meaning* is to be understood in relation to a particular domain or for a specific task. For instance, if one trains a model on business news, *debt* and *equity* might be placed close to each other, as referring to financing instruments. Also, in a sentiment analysis task, words associated with positive statements will correspond to vectors pointing in the same direction in that space.

So, word embeddings are a compact, and more efficient, representation of words through vectors of dimension anywhere between a few tens and a few hundreds. These dimensions capture a semantic similarity in a particular context. Once equipped with such a representation, one can then do basic vector combinations. For instance, by adding the vectors – trained on a sentiment corpus – corresponding to its words, one can infer the degree of positiveness of a given document.

Architectures to learn word embeddings vary. It can be a simple classification task for sentiment analysis, whereby one directly learns a model to retrieve the tone of a labelled series of documents. Or, for more generic tasks, one can reuse existing pre-trained models, with complex architectures trained on billions of words. Popular word embeddings are called *Word2vec*, *GloVe*, *ELMo* and *BERT*, which were all created after 2013.

Already at this stage of their development and despite their complexity, NLP algorithms can successfully tackle multiple tasks relevant to finance such as sentiment analysis of documents, topic modelling, text summarisation, text classification, and question answering. And the pace of discovery, partly due to ever-growing computational power and real-life applications, is not decelerating. We can expect significant breakthroughs in the near future.

16

THE FUTURE OF AI: WHAT WE CAN LOOK FORWARD TO

"We can only see a short distance ahead, but we can
see plenty there that needs to be done."

Alan Turing

While preparing for the inaugural Dartmouth conference in 1956
that officially launched AI as a discipline, the prominent organisers
expected that significant advances would be made in various areas of
interest in the space of two months.[157] Marvin Minsky, in his proposal
for the summer assignment, and talking about a neural machine, predicted that he would "have a model of such a machine fairly close to
the stage of programming in a computer". More than sixty years later,
the AI research community is still busy solving very similar problems
– natural language, neural networks, self-improvement, randomness
and creativity.

Looking ahead, when do experts expect *Artificial General Intelligence*
(AGI) to be reached? When will machines exhibit a level of generalisation similar to the one possessed by humans – and not just be good
at solving well-defined tasks, like in current *narrow AI*? The answers

---

157 (McCarthy, et al. 1955)

from respected researchers in the field range from one or two decades to many hundreds of years. Starting with the same set of knowledge, observing the same progress over the past decades, how can the specialists be so unsure?

One thing is certain is that we, human beings, are notoriously bad at making predictions, whether it is forecasting markets or company performance, but, equally, scientific progress. So, I will leave the outlook for intelligence in the hands of the futurists. It is more valuable to me to understand which fundamental questions still need to be answered to get closer to the ultimate goal of replicating human intelligence. Also, what key breakthroughs can we look forward to in the next few years?

I think the future of AI across industries is bright. There are undoubtedly important societal issues to be tackled along the way. As an example, technology will undoubtedly be transformative for jobs, especially for traditional professional or administrative workers. We are far from being able to mimic all our cognitive functions, but we are equally far from being able to replicate the most mundane manual tasks. And, we can be reassured by the fact that, even though machines have been taught to learn, we are wired, as a species, to adapt.

QUESTIONS THAT REMAIN UNANSWERED

There are some profound, almost philosophical, challenges when it comes to expanding our current AI capabilities to more general abilities. One of them is whether machines need physical bodies to progress much further. Once again, the target is human intelligence, which has a meaning only in relation to the physical world that exists around us. Many researchers believe that the next leap forward will come from adding perceptions to machines. So, machines will need sensing on top of their processing power. Humans do not just passively consume data. They interact with their environment, which in itself creates new experiences. Machines need to replicate this loop. A related question is whether the imperious necessity to protect our bodies plays an essential role in our thinking. Unless explicitly programmed, machines do not have the constraint of preserving their existence, which may be a fundamental difference with humans when making decisions.

Another crucial consideration of AI architecture is whether the most advanced technology currently at our disposal – deep learning – is sufficient to reach AGI. Is there another breakthrough that is required to solve true intelligence? Deep learning has been phenomenally efficient at solving incredibly complex tasks with results that were not anticipated a decade ago. But, for instance, can *consciousness* – that many take as a necessary attribute of truly intelligent machines – be emulated in a neural network? Is it just a mechanical feature that we could reproduce with sophisticated neural architecture, like the one in our brains, or does it require something else?

Some scientists, like Judea Pearl, argue that we rely too much on data and that consuming data passively cannot be the answer. In particular, Pearl believes that inferring causal relationships and making experiments are essential in our understanding of the world. In its current form, deep learning would not be sufficient. For him, our reasoning necessitates an ability to generate *counterfactuals* to develop new hypotheses and theories.

Another point that is still unclear is how to go past *narrow AI*. AI can perform very well at well-defined tasks, and most scientists think that expanding the list of tasks is just a matter of time. But, the community is still at a loss when figuring out how AI systems can solve more generic tasks, or, at the very least, expand their reach beyond the specific job they were designed for. The two answers, for the time being, are *transfer learning* and *ensemble learning*. *Transfer learning* revolves around reutilising the knowledge acquired on a particular task to solve a related problem. This is now commonly used in image processing, where object recognition learned on one specific type of object can be used to recognise other, but similar, objects without entirely retraining a new model. The technique may be promising but it is currently limited in its scope. *Ensemble learning* is the concept of running multiple models and aggregating them in some way to make better predictions. It is extensively used to improve model performance in a single task setting. But, it could be that learning to solve multiple problems – through different techniques – is a way to make machines more generic and capable in their scope.

NEXT MILESTONES

There is great excitement in the AI community when advances are made in answering these deeper questions which could have profound implications for currently out-of-reach problems. More prosaically, it is also interesting to see what lies ahead in the coming years. Deep learning architectures are still high on the research agenda. Models to efficiently process language and images, or data-generative models that produce new content, are only a few years old. *Explainability* and *interpretability* are also receiving much attention, as they are crucial for broader AI adoption and as a design tool for improved models.

Another area of research is the integration of prior knowledge in models. There used to be a healthy field of *symbolic AI* and *expert systems* attempting to encode human knowledge and expertise. This branch is now extinct and the dominant view is learning through data only. However, in many cases, a blend of human expertise and machine learning would be desirable. Expert inputs may be useful for accelerating learning, but also for improving performance. The encoding of *priors* in traditional machine learning models is still an art that needs improvement.

The other significant development to come is the further democratisation of AI tools. *AutoML* is one solution to this. Its objective is to bring powerful machine learning tools to everyone so that non-data scientists can experiment and run full pipelines without the complications of coding platforms. Being able to load a new dataset and to let the machine pick the best candidates to solve a given task will undoubtedly accelerate adoption and the reach of AI technology. There are still technical challenges involved in deploying the tools, but if advanced AI modelling becomes as ubiquitous as any other office tool, the concrete progress will be fast.

Shall we put the *singularity* in this list of upcoming changes? The singularity – also called *intelligence explosion* – is the point beyond which technological growth is so quick that it becomes uncontrollable and leads to an unpredictable phase for humanity. Through self-improvement, superintelligent agents far exceeding human intelligence will arise. While it is a perfectly valid theory – given the examples of exponential growth around us – we can safely say that it is not coming anytime soon. It certainly makes a good story for the futurists. But, in any case, keeping an eye on the possible unintended consequences of technological innovation is also a much-needed exercise to support sustainable progress.

BONUS: AI STORIES

"Science without conscience is but the ruin of the soul."

François Rabelais

In this chapter, I will offer a selection of AI stories. When thinking about a new type of technology, like AI, it is helpful to maintain an open and curious mind. AI takes its inspiration from many disciplines, and we could venture out in multiple directions. Keeping this open mind will undoubtedly enable a deeper understanding and foster creativity about the way that we can embrace a future with AI. In this book, I primarily focused on the fields of statistics, applied mathematics and computer science. Still, we could also think about this in terms of philosophy, metaphysics, logic, game theory, neuroscience, linguistics, and many others.

PLAYING GAMES

Let us start with a game. AI systems have become very good at playing board games. For a simple reason – they can play against themselves, without our help. This mechanism is called *self-play*, and cannot be better evidenced than in the computer program *AlphaZero*, developed by DeepMind in 2017. DeepMind – a subsidiary of Alphabet – has the ultimate ambition to solve AGI, but has been mostly known to the public for its achievements in board games (primarily, Atari games, chess and Go). The advantages of using games to approach intelligent behaviours are many but they primarily revolve around the existence of a well-defined environment. Games are the quintessential example of simulated conditions. The hope is that, in solving these complex games, one can better understand the intelligent mechanisms at play in less constrained situations.

The game of Go is considered the most complex game of all. On the 19x19 board, the number of admissible positions is well beyond human understanding, and about 90 orders of magnitude larger than the number of atoms in the universe.[158] The traditional way to play board games for computers has been to encode heuristics learned from top players, coupled with the computing ability to simulate many moves ahead. With these types of *clever* search, algorithms were able to rank the next move according to its probability to lead to an ultimate win. IBM's Deep Blue managed to beat Gary Kasparov, the then chess world champion, already in 1997. It relied on well-crafted rules, learned from experts. Despite its heavy reliance on computing power, it was closer to an *expert system* than what we call AI today.

However, chess is significantly simpler than the game of Go from a computational standpoint. A superhuman level at Go was not achieved before the defeat of international champion Lee Sedol by AlphaGo Zero in 2016. DeepMind had to design a particular architecture to do so. *Self-play* is a crucial part of it, as the AI system gets better by playing against itself over and over again. It is particularly true in the case of AlphaZero – the most advanced generation of these systems – which had no input from human players at all,[159] except for the knowledge of the rules.

---

158 The number – computed in 2016 – of *legal* positions is about $2 \times 10^{**}170$, compared to the usually accepted number of atoms in the universe, $10^{**}80$

159 AlphaGo Lee, the version that defeated Lee Sedol, was initially trained on a large database of around 30 million moves played by experts

The second key aspect is the search method, the *Monte-Carlo Tree Search* (MCTS), to evaluate the best next move. It involves letting the computer play *random* moves from the current board position. The program then assesses which next step is associated with the highest chance to win. Random moves are used because more exhaustive strategies are unthinkable due to the combinatorial explosion. Nevertheless, in the case of AlphaZero, the technique was adjusted to search for more intelligent paths than a random search. As training progresses, the AI system *takes note* of positions that are *more frequently visited*, in the sense that they have been learned as being associated with a higher chance of victory. To conduct its search at a given stage of the game, the algorithm will this time favour these positions of strength and search more extensively from these points onwards, before deciding on its next move. However, it will still preserve the possibility of observing more random positions to make sure that it regularly explores a broader space of possibilities.

The last ingredient in the algorithm is the neural network used to assess a given *state* of the game. The network is not only fed with the current board position, but also a history of previous moves. Also, it utilises CNNs – traditionally used for image recognition – to process the stack of pictures taken from the player's side. The network outputs a number of parameters characterising the value of a particular action at the next step.

In a nutshell, AlphaZero uses a combination of *reinforcement learning*, to assess strong moves based on future *rewards*, and *deep learning* technology, to understand the current *state* of the game. It also utilises its resources much more efficiently than before. For instance, it started beating its previous generation, AlphaGo Zero, after only 30 hours of training[160] – starting from absolute beginner where it had never played a single game of Go. Probably even more relevant for the generalisation of AI is the fact that the same architecture could reach superhuman performance in a matter of hours at the games of chess and shogi, easily beating the current best engines. Once again, AlphaZero did not know how to play these games at inception and did not receive any expert input.

At a more metaphysical level, these machines have exhibited traits that we would commonly associate with human intelligence. The algorithms came up with winning strategies that no human player had ever discovered, despite the thousands of years of knowledge in playing these games. There was creativity in some of the games too. For instance, in game 2 between Lee Sedol and AlphaGo Zero, the machine played a bizarre move according to professional Go players. It was something that no human player would ever do, but it turned out to be a move of beauty and genius.

DeepMind's David Silver noted that the way the machine plays now forms an integral part of the professional players' training at the games of chess and Go. Having developed its own intuition – away from human experience – the AI system has expanded the limits of the game. It may leave us pondering what this new form of intelligence truly is.

THE SIMULATION ARGUMENT

Fortunately, the prospect of machines taking over at board games is not as frightening as some form of *singularity* where the human race could be enslaved by superintelligent agents. Despite their vast range of possible combinations, these games have clear boundaries.

---

160 It is worth noting that the algorithm could use specialised hardware from Google, which was multiple orders of magnitude more powerful than a personal computer

Their world is just an 8x8 or 19x19 board with simple rules. Also, chess, Go, and other similar games are a particular class of games, where there is *perfect information*. There is no randomness involved, meaning that the same moves will always lead to the same state of the game.

This does not look much like the world we live in. However, for the AI doomsayers, there is an argument worth contemplating. The likes of Elon Musk claim that there is a very high chance that we live in a *simulation*, meaning that a singularity moment has already happened. It is easy to dismiss this argument for many reasons: the proponents of such a theory like to provoke, or they enjoy the publicity associated with it, or they like to portray a dystopian view of the world coming from excessive consumption of science fiction.

In reality, the theory of the *simulation argument* comes from a well-respected philosopher and academic in the field of AI. Nick Bostrom is the founding director of the Future of Humanity Institute at the University of Oxford. The so-called argument is actually not conclusive and is better characterised as a trilemma. It stipulates that one of three hypotheses has to be true. To understand them, one needs first to define *technological maturity*. It is an advanced level of technological progress whereby a posthuman civilisation would have the ability to run a detailed simulation of their forebears – an *ancestor civilisation* – only using a fraction of their resources.

The first hypothesis says that all human-level civilisations would have become extinct before they reach technological maturity. Or, secondly, all civilisations with technological maturity would have lost interest in running ancestor simulations. Or, thirdly, there is a very high proportion of us, with our kinds of experiences, who live in a simulation. Once again, only one of these three propositions can be true.

For instance, one may believe that there must be at least one civilisation that is able to reach, at some point, a technological level enabling it to simulate the world as we know it with enough granularity and realism. And one may also assume that there is enough divergence across – and within – civilisations to imagine that, with such technological power, some agents might be interested in running these ancestor simulations. Otherwise, this would imply that there is a very high degree of similarity within these advanced civilisations. If one thinks that both affirmations are true – that such civilisations may exist at some point and that some individuals within them may be interested in running such simulations – then we are most likely living in a simulation, hence the not-so-absurd *simulation hypothesis*.

There are many considerations in this debate. At this stage of our scientific development, can we even picture what it means to run such advanced simulations? Do we even know if there are no physical limitations that cannot be overcome? Does it tie in with our understanding of *consciousness*? Do we also want to know if the simulation hypothesis is correct? Interestingly, some physicists are trying to figure out what measurements are required to conclude whether we are in a simulation or not – even possibly from within a simulation. Experts are worried that knowing that we live in a simulation would dramatically affect the fabric of our societies. Would we behave the same or consider the meaning of life in the same way, if all this was a simulation, at the mercy of being interrupted at any time by its creators?

I will now let you, the reader, decide which probability to attribute to each hypothesis. We may have deviated a bit too much from our initial subject of AI in finance, which now looks quite pedestrian in the light of the simulation hypothesis.

SELECTED ABBREVIATIONS

AGI	Artificial General Intelligence
AI	Artificial Intelligence
ANN	Artificial Neural Network
API	Application Programming Interface
AutoML	Automated Machine Learning
CDAO	Chief Data & Analytics Officer
CDO	Chief Data Officer
CNN	Convolutional Neural Network
DL	Deep Learning
EDA	Exploratory Data Analysis
GAN	Generative Adversarial Network
LSTM	Long Short-Term Memory
ML	Machine Learning
MLP	MultiLayer Perceptron
NLP	Natural Language Processing
RMSE	Root Mean Square Error
RNN	Recurrent Neural Network
ROC	Receiver Operating Characteristic
SVM	Support Vector Machine
XAI	eXplainable AI

APPENDIX: FURTHER READING

GENERAL KNOWLEDGE

Melanie Mitchell's recent book is an incredibly clear introduction to
  AI:
Artificial Intelligence: A Guide for Thinking Humans by Melanie
  Mitchell

This series of interviews by Martin Ford is a useful aid to understanding the thought-process of the current leading AI experts:
Architects of Intelligence by Martin Ford

MORE ADVANCED CONSIDERATIONS

These three books, by world-leading experts, focus on superintelli-
  gence, the future of AI and humanity:
Human Compatible: Artificial Intelligence and the Problem of Control
  by Stuart Russell
Superintelligence: Paths, Dangers, Strategies by Nick Bostrom
Rebooting AI by Gary Marcus, Ernest Davis

On the more specific question of causality in AI, Turing Award recipient Judea Pearl wrote this inspiring book:
The Book of Why by Judea Pearl, Dana Mackenzie

TECHNICAL BOOKS

This book is the most concise introduction to modelling in machine learning:

The Hundred-Page Machine Learning Book by Andruiy Brkov

These three books are classic textbooks covering various areas of the theory in machine learning:

The Elements of Statistical Learning by Trevor Hastie, Robert Tibshirani, Jerome Friedman

Artificial Intelligence: A Modern Approach by Stuart Russell, Peter Norvig

Deep Learning by Ian Goodfellow, Yoshua Bengio, Aaron Courville

CODING BOOKS

For those interested in practising machine learning, these two books are a must-have:

Hands-On Machine Learning with Scikit-Learn and TensorFlow (2nd Edition) by Aurélien Géron

Deep Learning with Python by François Chollet

LIST OF FIGURES

REFERENCES

2018. "Ant Financial extends dominance in Chinese online finance." *ft.com*. 17 5. https://www.ft.com/content/fde8fe0c-5830-11e8-b8b2-d6ceb45fa9d0.

Bank of England; Financial Conduct Authority. 2019. "Machine learning in UK financial services." 10. https://www.fca.org.uk/publication/research/research-note-on-machine-learning-in-uk-financial-services.pdf.

2020. "Bank research embraces alternative data." *euromoney.com*. 20 4. https://www.euromoney.com/article/b1l63f2yrl2cmp/bank-research-embraces-alternative-data.

Banko, Michele, and Eric Brill. 2001. "Scaling to very very large corpora for natural language disambiguation." *Proceedings of the 39th annual meeting of the Association for Computational Linguistics.* 26–33.

Bostrom, Nick. 2003. "Ethical issues in advanced artificial intelligence." In *Science Fiction and Philosophy: From Time Travel to Superintelligence*, 277–284.

—. 2014. *Superintelligence: Paths, Dangers, Strategies.* Oxford University Press.

Burkov, Andriy. 2019. *The Hundred-Page Machine Learning Book.* Andriy Burkov.

Calvano, Emilio, Giacomo Calzolari, Vincenzo Denicolò, and Sergio Pastorello. 2019. "Artificial intelligence, algorithmic pricing and collusion." *Algorithmic Pricing and Collusion.*

Cauchy, Augustin-Louis. 1847. "Méthode générale pour la résolution des systemes d'équations simultanées." *Comptes Rendus de l'Academie des Sciences*, 536–538.

Chollet, François. 2017. *Deep Learning with Python*. Manning Publications.

Chollet, François. 2019. *On the measure of intelligence*. arXiv preprint arXiv:1911.01547.

Ford, Martin. 2018. *Architects of Intelligence: The Truth about AI from the People Building It*. Packt Publishing Ltd.

Friedman, Jerome, Trevor Hastie, and Robert Tibshirani. 2001. *The Elements of Statistical Learning*. New York: Springer.

Géron, Aurélien. 2019. *Hands-On Machine Learning with Scikit-Learn, Keras, and TensorFlow: Concepts, Tools, and Techniques to Build Intelligent Systems*. O'Reilly Media.

Goodfellow, Ian, Yoshua Bengio, Aaron Courville, and Yoshua Bengio. 2016. *Deep Learning*. Cambridge: MIT Press.

Groysberg, Boris, Jeremiah Lee, Jesse Price, and J. Cheng. 2018. "The leader's guide to corporate culture." *Harvard Business Review* 96 (1): 44–52.

Hofstadter, Douglas R. 1979. *Gödel, Escher, Bach: An Eternal Golden Braid*. New York: Basic Books.

Hubel, David H., and Torsten N. Wiesel. 1968. "Receptive fields and functional architecture of monkey striate cortex." *The Journal of Physiology* 195 (1): 215–243.

Hutson, Matthew. 2018. "Artificial intelligence faces reproducibility crisis." *Science* 359 (6377): 725–726.

IBM Marketing Cloud. 2017. "10 Key Marketing Trends for 2017 and Ideas for Exceeding Customer Expectations." ftp://ftp.www.ibm.com/software/in/pdf/10_Key_Marketing_Trends_for_2017.pdf.

2019. "It's official: Google has achieved quantum supremacy." *newscientist.com*. 23 10. https://www.newscientist.com/article/2220968-its-official-google-has-achieved-quantum-supremacy/.

Jia, Yuping, Laurence Van Lent, and Yachang Zeng. 2014. "Masculinity, testosterone, and financial misreporting." *Journal of Accounting Research* 52 (5): 1195–1246.

Kahneman, Daniel, and Amos Tversky. 1973. "On the psychology of prediction." *Psychological Review* 80 (4): 237.

Lin, Henry W., Max Tegmark, and David Rolnick. 2017. "Why does deep and cheap learning work so well?." *Journal of Statistical Physics* 168 (6): 1223–1247.

Marcus, Gary, and Ernest Davis. 2019. *Rebooting AI: Building Artificial Intelligence We Can Trust.* Ballantine Books Inc.

Mayew, William J., and Mohan Venkatachalam. 2012. "The power of voice: Managerial affective states and future firm performance." *The Journal of Finance* 67 (1): 1–43.

McCarthy, John, Marvin Minsky, Nathan Rochester, and Claude Shannon. 1955. "A Proposal for the Dartmouth Summer Research Project on Artificial Intelligence." August. http://raysolomonoff.com/dartmouth/boxa/dart564props.pdf.

McKinsey & Company. 2018. "Banks in the changing world of financial intermediation." 6 11. https://www.mckinsey.com/industries/financial-services/our-insights/banks-in-the-changing-world-of-financial-intermediation.

2020. "Mercer's theorem." *en.wikipedia.org.* https://en.wikipedia.org/wiki/Mercer%27s_theorem.

Mitchell, Melanie. 2019. *Artificial Intelligence: A Guide for Thinking Humans.* Penguin UK.

Mitchell, Tom M. 1997. *Machine Learning.* McGraw Hill.

MMC Ventures. 2019. "The State of AI 2019: Divergence." https://www.stateofai2019.com/.

Moore, Gordon E. 1965. "Cramming more components onto integrated circuits." https://newsroom.intel.com/wp-content/uploads/sites/11/2018/05/moores-law-electronics.pdf.

2020. "Moore's law." *en.wikipedia.org*. https://en.wikipedia.org/wiki/Moore%27s_law.

Pearl, Judea. 2019. "The seven tools of causal inference, with reflections on machine learning." *Communications of the ACM* 62 (3): 54–60.

Pearl, Judea, and Dana Mackenzie. 2019. *The Book of Why: The New Science of Cause and Effect.* Penguin.

Phillips, Mary Ellen, Norma L. Nielson, and Carol E. Brown. 1992. "An evaluation of expert systems." *Journal of Financial Counseling and Planning* 3 (1).

Pinkus, Allan. 1999. "Approximation theory of the MLP model in neural networks." *Acta numerica* 8 (1): 143–195.

2006. "Promise of AI not so bright." *washingtontimes.com*. 13 4. https://www.washingtontimes.com/news/2006/apr/13/20060413-105217-7645r/.

Quandl Inc. 2020. *https://www.quandl.com/*.

Randal S. Olson, William La Cava, Zairah Mustahsan, Akshay Varik and Jason H. Moore. 2018. "Data-driven advice for applying machine learning to bioinformatics problems." *Proceedings of the Pacific Symposium.* 192–203.

Russell, Stuart. 2019. *Human Compatible: Artificial Intelligence and the Problem of Control.* Penguin.

Russell, Stuart, and Peter Norvig. 2020. *Artificial Intelligence: A Modern Approach (Fourth Edition).* Pearson.

Schapire, Robert E., and Yoav Freund. 2012. *Boosting: Foundations and Algorithms. Adaptive Computation and Machine Learning.* Cambridge: MIT Press.

Strohmeier, Martin, Matthew Smith, Vincent Lenders, and Ivan Martinovic. 2018. "The real first class? Inferring confidential corporate mergers and government relations from air traffic communication." *IEEE European Symposium on Security and Privacy (EuroS&P).* IEEE. 107–121.

Temin, Peter. 2002. "Price behavior in ancient Babylon." *Explorations in Economic History* 39 (1): 46-60.

Teoh, Siew Hong, Lin Peng, Yakun Wang, and Jiawen Yan. 2019. "Face Value: Do Perceived-Facial Traits Matter for Sell-side Analysts?"

2009. "The BellKor Solution to the Netflix Grand Prize." 8. https://www.netflixprize.com/assets/GrandPrize2009_BPC_BellKor.pdf.

The European Parliament and the Council. 2016. "Regulation (EU) 2016/679 of the European Parliament and of the Council of 27 April 2016 on the protection of natural persons with regard to the processing of personal data and on the free movement of such data, and repealing Directive 95/46/EC." 27 4. http://data.europa.eu/eli/reg/2016/679/2016-05-04.

1973. *The Lighthill debate on Artificial Intelligence: "The general purpose robot is a mirage"*. https://www.youtube.com/watch?v=03p2CADwGF8.

1885. *The Politics of Aristotle*. Vol. 1. Clarendon.

n.d. *This person does not exist.* https://thispersondoesnotexist.com/.

Turing, Alan M. 2009. "Computing machinery and intelligence." In *Parsing the Turing Test*, 23–65. Dordrecht: Springer.

Weber, Roger, and Klemens Böhm. 2000. "Trading quality for time with nearest-neighbor search." *International Conference on Extending Database Technology.* Berlin: Springer. 21–35.

2018. "Why millennials are driving cashless revolution in China." *ft.com.* 17 7. https://www.ft.com/content/539e39b8-851b-11e8-a29d-73e3d454535d.

Zhu, Christina. 2019. "Big data as a governance mechanism." *The Review of Financial Studies* 32 (5): 2021–2061.

ACKNOWLEDGMENTS

This book is mostly inspired by the numerous conversations I have had over the years with financial professionals from all industries, whether at work or outside work. Many friends, colleagues or clients will undoubtedly recognise some of the book topics as the basis of our discussions. I cannot realistically thank hundreds of people for helping me fine-tune my arguments and views, so please accept my collective appreciation.

However, there is one person that I would like to mention by name. Ashwin Parameswaran has been kind enough to review the entire book and give me his valuable comments. You could say he is an expert in finance and technology, which is convenient given the subject of the book. Yet, when discussing with Ashwin, one needs to be prepared to talk in the same conversation about risk retention in securitisation, Eastern philosophy, multi-agent game theory, system resilience in wildfires, Python procedures, the Austrian school of economics, or some obscure form of meditation. François Rabelais would certainly be pleased with the extent of his knowledge in our current age, but I am just happy to call him my friend.

I would also like to thank my family, in particular my parents and children. In many cases, they were the guinea pigs of my attempts to explain some of the concepts exposed in this book. I do apologise for being so obsessed with the subject. Now that the writing is over, I hope that I can join some lighter conversations too. I also observed multiple times my youngest son trying to understand how he was acquiring new pieces of knowledge. It just confirmed how far we still have to go to replicate our marvellous brain in its cognitive abilities.

Lastly, a special mention goes to my wife, Kristina. I took away many hours of family life to write this book. She is always incredibly supportive when I come up with new ideas. She even pretended to be proud when I told her I was starting a book on artificial intelligence and finance. Her continuous encouragement was crucial when, at times, this endeavour seemed particularly taxing.

INDEX